Praise for *Software by Numbers*

"Mark Denne and Jane Cleland-Hu[...] [...] [...] cant new contribution to value-based, [...] [...]ware engineering. People and organizations looking for specific techniques to increase the business value of their software-intensive systems will find its Minimum Marketable Features and Incremental funding methodology techniques highly cost-effective to apply."

—BARRY BOEHM, PH.D.
Director, USC Center for Software Engineering
Creator of COCOMO and Spiral Model

"To succeed in today's IT environment we can no longer ignore the gap that exists between the vocabulary and value systems of business stakeholders and those of software developers. Successful software projects must not only be delivered on time and within budget, but must fulfill organizational objectives and bring meaningful financial rewards. This can only be accomplished by managing business strategies as an integral part of the software development process. This book addresses the need head-on with analytical techniques, concepts, and tools to ensure that your corporation's software investment does not fall into the gap of cost overruns, finger pointing, late delivery, and feature irrelevancy!"

—CARL K. CHANG, PH.D.
President IEEE Computer Society, 2004
Professor and Chair, Computer Science Department, Iowa State University

"An exciting new approach to software development that promises to deliver revenue sooner by applying analytical math to feature prioritization, can be snapped onto either of the leading industry methodologies, and provides obvious opportunity for embracing the business in the feature-vetting part of the process."

—RON LICHTY
Macromedia product manager for enterprise solutions
and recent emigre from Fortune 500 IT

"*Software by Numbers* offers a rational approach to the often contentious process of feature prioritization by applying an objective mathematic framework to the process. Looking at prioritization based on ROI offers great opportunity for creating a dialogue between IT and business."

—LATICIA MILLER
Deloitte Consulting
Project manager for business process outsourcing

About Prentice Hall Professional Technical Reference

With origins reaching back to the industry's first computer science publishing program in the 1960s, and formally launched as its own imprint in 1986, Prentice Hall Professional Technical Reference (PH PTR) has developed into the leading provider of technical books in the world today. Our editors now publish over 200 books annually, authored by leaders in the fields of computing, engineering, and business.

Our roots are firmly planted in the soil that gave rise to the technical revolution. Our bookshelf contains many of the industry's computing and engineering classics: Kernighan and Ritchie's *C Programming Language*, Nemeth's *UNIX System Adminstration Handbook*, Horstmann's *Core Java*, and Johnson's *High-Speed Digital Design*.

PH PTR acknowledges its auspicious beginnings while it looks to the future for inspiration. We continue to evolve and break new ground in publishing by providing today's professionals with tomorrow's solutions.

PRENTICE
HALL
PTR

SOFTWARE
BY NUMBERS

Low-Risk, High-Return Development

Mark Denne
Jane Cleland-Huang

PRENTICE
HALL
PTR

PRENTICE HALL
Professional Technical Reference
Upper Saddle River, New Jersey 07458
www.phptr.com

Prentice Hall PTR offers excellent discounts on this book when ordered in quantity for bulk purchases or special sales. For more information, please contact: U.S. Corporate and Government Sales, 1-800-382-3419, corpsales@pearsontechgroup.com. For sales outside of the U.S., please contact: International Sales, 1-317-581-3793, international@pearsontechgroup.com.

Executive Editor: *Gregory G. Doench*
Cover Design Director: *Jerry Votta*
Editorial Assistant: *Brandt Kenna*
Manufacturing Manager: *Alexis R. Heydt-Long*
Marketing Manager: *Debby vanDijk*

Sun Microsystems Press:
Publisher: *Myrna Rivera*

First Printing

ISBN 0-13-140728-7

Sun Microsystems Press
A Prentice Hall Title

Contents

Preface   *xiii*

Chapter 1
Software Development after dot.com   *1*

Software Development Is Easy   *1*

There's a Method to the Madness   *3*

If History Teaches Us Anything . . .   *3*

Minimum Marketable Feature   *5*

MMF Selection   *6*

Opening the Black Box of Software Development   *7*

Risk Control   *8*

Sigma Techniques   *9*

Measurable Customer Requirements   *10*
Data-Backed Decision Making   *10*
Incorporating the Voice of the Customer   *10*
Challenging the Status Quo   *10*
Span Organizational Structures   *10*
Continuously Measurable Progress   *11*

Summary   *11*

References   *12*

Chapter 2
The New ROI

Applications and ROIs   13

Why ROIs Matter   14

The Business Case   15

Cash Flow Projections   15

Payback Time   16

Present Value of Future Money   17

Net Present Value   17

Breakeven Time   18

Internal Rate of Return   18

Summary of the Terms   19

An Example   19

Incorporating MMFs into the Financial Case   22

Comparing the MMF-based ROI with the Classic ROI   24

Taking the Risks into Account   24

The Impact of MMF Ordering   25

Summary   25

References   25

Chapter 3
Identifying and Valuing Marketable Features

Incremental Funding Methodology   27

Minimum Marketable Features   28

Candidate MMFs   30

Determining the Value of an MMF   31

Development and Delivery Precursors   37

The MMF Precedence Graph   38

Architectural Precursors   40

Summary   *40*

References   *40*

Chapter 4
Incremental Architecture   *43*

The Place of Architecture   *43*

Architecture versus Rules   *44*

The Problem with Architecture   *45*

Pieces of the Pattern   *46*

A Value-Driven Approach   *47*

The Codependency of Architecture   *48*

Taking Architecture in Easy Stages   *49*

A Different Decomposition   *50*

One-to-Many Dependencies in Architecture   *53*

Architectural Coherency   *54*

Multiple Inheritance in Architecture   *55*

Spiral Architecture   *57*

Summary   *58*

References   *58*

Chapter 5
IFM Sequencing Strategies   *61*

Delivering Valued Features   *61*

Cost versus Value Analysis   *62*

Cost-Benefit Analysis of an MMF Delivery Sequence   *63*

The Complexity of the Task   *66*

MMF Sequencing Strategies   *67*

The Greedy Approach   *67*

A Simple Look-Ahead Approach   *69*

The Weighted Look-Ahead Approach   *73*

Sequencing MMFs and AEs   *74*

Risk Mitigation   *76*

Iterating the Sequencing Decision   *76*

Summary   *77*

References   *77*

Chapter 6

MMF Categories and Parallel Development   *79*

The Impact of MMF Behavior   *79*

Time-Sensitive Delivery   *81*

Exponential Growth Patterns   *82*

Concurrent Development   *83*

Summary   *88*

References   *88*

Chapter 7

Managing Intangibles   *89*

Apples and Oranges: Dealing with Intangibles   *89*

Managing Intangibles   *90*

A Pairwise Approach to Quantifying Intangibles   *92*

Step 1: Identify a Set of Gauges   *92*
Step 2: Construct a Pairwise Comparison Table   *94*
Step 3: Make Pairwise Comparisons   *94*
Step 4: Calculate Equivalent SANPVs   *95*

Hybrid MMFs   *97*

The Impact of Intangibles on the Cost-Benefits Analysis   *97*

Baseline NPV   *99*

Potential NPV   *99*

Lost Opportunity Costs   *100*

Summary   *101*

References   *102*

Chapter 8

IFM and the Unified Process   *103*

Introduction   *103*

Inception   *105*

Define the Vision Statement   *106*
Define the Business Case   *106*
Elicit MMFs   *106*
Decompose MMFs into Use Cases   *107*
Construct an MMF Graph   *108*
Identify Major Risks Associated with Each MMF   *108*
Develop a Project Glossary   *109*
The Lifecycle Objective Milestone   *109*

Elaboration   *110*

Architectural Selection   *110*
Cost and Effort Estimation   *111*
The Lifecycle Architecture Milestone   *112*

MMF Development and Delivery   *113*

MMF Sequencing   *113*
NPV Milestone   *114*

MMF Design   *114*

Elicit Requirements   *115*
Design   *115*
MMF Project Plan   *115*
Feature Design Milestone   *116*

MMF Construction   *116*

Feature Operational Capability   *117*
MMF Transition   *118*
Feature Release Milestone   *118*

MMF Selection Revisited   *119*

Summary   *119*
References   *119*

Chapter 9
IFM and Agile Development   *121*

The Challenges   *121*
Incremental Development the Agile Way   *123*
Clustering User Stories into MMFs   *124*
Release Planning: Bundling User Stories in Releases   *127*
Assessing the NPV of the Release Plan   *129*
Release Planning Meeting   *131*
The Architecture Question   *132*
Simplest versus Look-Ahead Solution   *134*
Other Agile Development Environments   *139*
   Feature-driven Development   *140*
SCRUM   *142*
Summary   *143*
References   *143*

Chapter 10
Informed Decision Making   *145*

A Collaborative Approach   *145*
Getting a Project Funded   *146*
Manipulating Project Characteristics   *149*
The IFM Window   *151*
Implementing IFM Processes   *152*
The Impact of IFM Strategies on Commercial Frameworks   *153*
How Management Benefits from IFM   *155*
When Projects Go Wrong   *155*

Where Next? *157*

Summary *157*

References *158*

Chapter 11

A Case Study: IFM in Action *159*

Introduction *159*

IFM Element Definition Phase *160*

  Selecting MMFs *160*

  Defining MMF Strands *161*

  Eliciting Architectural Elements *161*

  Defining Architectural Dependencies *163*

  Construct IFM Precedence Graph *163*

Financial Phase *164*

Computation Phase *166*

  Sequence-Adjusted NPVs *166*

  Sequence Selection *168*

  The Greedy Heuristic *168*

  The IFM Heuristic *170*

Measuring the Effectiveness of the IFM Heuristic *173*

ROI Analysis *175*

Cash Flow and Breakeven Time *176*

  Concurrent Development *177*

Summary *180*

Appendix A *183*

Appendix B *186*

Index *187*

Preface

"Absolutely! You must write the book!"

Such was the enthusiastic response of my manager, Stu Stern, Vice President of Sun Professional Services, to the idea of a book that would draw on the latest ideas in application development methodologies and apply them primarily for financial rather than technological benefit.

For all our efforts and successes in creating development methodologies, only a few practitioners have realized the potential for using these techniques to maximize financial return. And yet financial return is usually the enduring metric of success in software development, at least in the commercial world.

This book draws on several years of experience in winning competitive contracts for systems integration and application development projects. Although winning such deals is unquestionably about using innovation to outflank the competition, it's also about getting the money right. The price has to be within the customer's budget, the development cost has to be low enough for the bidder to make a good margin, and the margin has to be justified against the risk. There's nothing new in those ideas; they are true for any competitive procurement.

What is different about software development is that we're only just learning to understand value creation. The most common view is that software development incurs risks and costs. Despite this, even the most hardened, risk-averse development house would recognize that software carries implicit value. If that value were not there, no one would pay to have software developed. Unfortunately, all of the creative and business energies of the development organization are normally focused on reducing cost and risk. This is as true in the bid phase as in the implementation phase. The developer applies the latest software methodologies, institutes the latest project management strategies, and constantly evolves risk mitigation techniques, primarily to do just one thing: control cost.

Ironically, most of this activity is invisible to the customer, and the customer is rarely a part of the conversations that lead to the critical project decisions in these areas.

In the 1990s, I worked on a large competitive procurement for a Southeast Asian government. The nature of the project was such that differentiation through technical innovation was very limited because the evaluation parameters were just too tightly tied down. We needed a different way to win. It eventually occurred to me that if we optimized the time at which value was returned to the customer, instead of concentrating only on controlling risk and cost, we might be able to use that approach to present a uniquely differentiated value proposition. By reanalyzing and recategorizing the customer's requirements in terms of units of value, we found that we could indeed adjust the development sequence so that we delivered real value faster than if we'd optimized for total cost. At the same time we could amortize the cost into more manageable portions, each part of which had accountability for its returns.

The impact for the customer was dramatic. The approach was able to significantly reduce the borrowing line and interest payments, facilitate the earlier release of the product to market, and create a much cleaner modularity from a financial perspective.

The merchant banks needed to recompute the project finance numbers, the developers needed to understand why we were apparently reordering the customer's requirements, and the customers, of course, needed to see, understand, and compute for themselves the benefits of this approach. Very unusual conversations took place during this time. Developers became involved in conversations with bankers about return on investment. Project managers traded spreadsheets with financiers and investors. Analysts measured architectures in terms of "time to value" rather than functional efficiency. At the end of the process, instead of two presentations to the customer, one on the technology and one on the finances, we gave just one presentation covering both, with all sides of the team represented. We won the day, and the business!

Such was the genesis of incrementally funded software development, which later gave birth to the incremental funding methodology (IFM) outlined in this book. Naturally, the idea took many months to bring to fruition. The gestation of any idea is an unpredictable process. It's rarely clear exactly what will emerge until it does. Although the idea of incrementally funded software had shown some early signs of success, it needed to be more comprehensively proven. I was privileged to take over the management of Sun Microsystems' New York "Java Center" in late 1999. The Java Center is Sun's global Java Consultancy practice, and provides architecture and design expertise to customers creating solutions in Java and J2EE. It was quickly apparent that by writing the embryonic IFM concepts into proposals for application development work, we were able to capture and successfully deliver several very large engagements, particularly with finance industry clients. However we learned that incremental funding and the early release of value are critically dependent on the nature of the requirements and on their ability to be reconfigured for value optimization. Requirements engineering is a discipline in itself, and I was fortunate to know an expert in this field.

My co-author is Jane Cleland-Huang, assistant professor of Computer Science at DePaul University in Chicago. I first met Jane when we were both 16 and growing up in England. We had a common interest in supporting aid organizations for the Third World and met at a 24-hour sponsored "starve-in" in the small town of Wimborne Minster in Dorset, England. At that time I had just learned to write Fortran IV programs on punched cards and run them through the batch terminal at the local technical college after school. Jane's interest in programming developed later when she began working for an international relief organization. In the meantime, we went to the same church, had several friends in common, and began a lifelong friendship that survived university, relief work assignments in different countries, and, eventually, Jane's departure to live in Chicago. Some time later while I was living and working in San Francisco, I flew to Chicago and invited Jane to meet me at the O'Hare Airport Hilton to propose that we write this book together. To my great delight, she agreed. Her background and experience are pivotal to this book in every sense.

We owe a debt to many people in the production of this book. For my part I must first thank my manager, Cheryln Chin, Vice President of Software Services at Sun Microsystems, for allowing me the time and space to produce this work. I need also to thank Albert Lam, previously regional manager of Sun Professional Services Asia South, now regional manager of Apple Computer in Singapore, for trusting my instincts and allowing me to prototype the IFM ideas on one of his most important customers. My thanks also go to Cecilia Lam, previously with the Arab Malaysian Merchant Bank and now with Cap Gemini Ernst & Young Singapore, for her financial insight and support in the early use of IFM and for her review comments on the book in recent months. We owe an unequalled debt of thanks to Ron Lichty of Macromedia for his detailed review of the drafts and for many helpful suggestions for revision and correction. I must also take this opportunity to profusely thank Stu and Alison Stern for the loan of their wonderful vacation home high in the Rocky Mountains of Colorado as a base to review the copy edits.

M.D.

When Mark first approached me about co-authoring this book I was immediately intrigued with the idea because the concepts of IFM closely matched my own research interests in requirements engineering and software development processes. Both Mark and I felt that the blend of his practical experience with my academic background would provide the balance needed for writing the book.

With Mark living in San Francisco and me in Chicago, the actual writing of the book involved several marathon book sessions in Chicago, many long hours on the phone, and of course hundreds of inevitable e-mails to discuss concepts related to IFM principles and metrics; incremental architecture needed to improve financial viability of a project; the impact of intangibles upon the sequencing process; and many other related issues.

We encountered several challenges along the way. The most significant one was to develop IFM heuristics and principles needed to define a roadmap for others to follow, so that our readers would be able to optimize the value of their own incrementally funded software projects. We explored several different approaches, each time comparing the results against the results of a brute-force approach to optimizing a project's value, until we identified the IFM heuristic described in this book that we found to perform consistently well. Our final challenge was in choosing a suitable title that would capture the synergism between software development and financial management.

Despite long lists of ideas, extensive phone calls with our editor Greg Doench, and very creative ideas from my children, whose enthusiasm was no doubt in part due to the offer of $10 to anyone who thought up a suitable title, the book had yet to be named!

In desperation I launched a "competition" among DePaul faculty members, offering a free lunch for two at a local restaurant for whomever proposed the title that was finally selected. This produced an enthusiastic response with suggestions such as "Paying by the Feature," "If You Can't Fund It Don't Code It!," "Form Follows Funding," and "Paying for Projects the Smart Way." Although each of these suggestions captured an important part of the book's topic, we were still not satisfied that any of these titles fully represented its primary message.

Finally, at the eleventh hour, while relaxing over a glass of Matanzas Creek Sauvignon Blanc, Mark thought up the idea of *Software by Numbers*. The analogy was immediately obvious and depicted the ability to deconstruct a software development project into pieces, and sequence them according to the value they would return. Even without the analogy to paint-by-numbers kits, the title still captured the essence of the book. Software development should integrate and consider project metrics that assess its financial impact.

In closing I should say that writing this book has been an adventure. The book that we originally planned to write during our initial meeting at the Hilton Hotel evolved into something entirely different. What remained was Mark's original idea of the incremental funding methodology. What changed was our limited thinking that IFM was a methodology in itself. We grew to understand that these ideas and principles were applicable to a broad spectrum of software development processes. The book therefore evolved from a distinct methodology into an approach that is broadly applicable within both traditional and agile development environments.

On my part, I would like to thank Dr. Massimo DiPierro, Visiting Assistant Professor at DePaul and President of MetaCryption for his review of the algorithmic content of the book. We thank Greg Truex from NorthStar Credit Union and David Schmelzer from Bank One, whose expertise in both the banking industry and software development provided a unique perspective that resulted in invaluable feedback. We also thank Laticia Miller, Senior Consultant with Deloitte Consulting, and Chris Jones from DePaul University for their input and review of our earlier materials, and Michael Dain for providing the example used in the chapter on intangibles.

Our thanks go to Luigi Guadagno, a cofounder of the Chicago Agile Developers group (CHAD), who offered knowledgeable insight into the agile development process, and to Kent Beck for sharing his perspective on applying IFM principles to eXtreme Programming and for his challenge to demonstrate the application of IFM to the agile development process. We also thank Dr. Michael Fries, Visiting Assistant Professor at DePaul, and Sridevi Kalidindi for their contribution to the empirical study reported on the companion Web site at http://www.softwarebynumbers.org.

In addition I would like to thank five members of my undergraduate computer science capstone class—Agneesh Banerjee, Huyen Nguyen, Huzaifa Tapal, Kaleeta Wright, and Robert Velazquez—who developed an early prototype of the IFM tool, and the master's students from the fall 2002 and spring 2003 courses, Advanced Topics in Systems Development, for their involvement in the project and for their informative feedback.

Last but not least I would like to thank all the DePaul faculty members who participated in our "book naming contest."

J.C.-H.

Our thanks also go to our Prentice Hall editor Greg Doench, to Sun Microsystems Press coordinator Myrna Rivera, and to Jennifer Lundburg, our marketing manager at Prentice Hall.

Our hope in writing this book is that it will impart insight to developers, managers, business executives, and venture investors. If it provides a common vocabulary all parties can use to exchange ideas with the objective of enhancing the financial success and reducing the risk of application development projects, it will have fulfilled its primary purpose. To further help you, the book has a companion Web site at http://www.softwarebynumbers.org, at which you can find additional information and downloadable tools to help you on your way.

We trust you will find the chapters that follow challenging, useful, and enjoyable. We would welcome your feedback via the Web site.

May all your software projects be both successful and profitable!

Dedication

To Nathan, Luke, and Alex
—Mark Denne

To Harold, Tori, Melissa, and Philip
—Jane Cleland-Huang

Software Development after dot.com

Now that the dot.com bubble has burst, new and radical approaches to software development are needed to respond to business demands for shorter investment periods, faster time to market, and increased operational agility. It's time to open the black box of technologically driven development methodologies and recognize that software creation is fundamentally a value creation process. It's time to subject software creation to the same detailed financial scrutiny and accountability received by any other value creation process.■

Software Development Is Easy

"Software development is easy" is the bold claim of the integrated development environment (IDE) manufacturers of the early 21st century[1]. Just learn the language, learn the tools, and use our IDE, and you too can produce quality software. It'll be on time, within budget, self-documenting. It'll be first to market in the fiercely competitive world of Internet time. And it'll make money, lots of money.

Sadly, none of this is true.

Countless reports of cancelled or incomplete projects have sent a clear message that software development can be an expensive and risky endeavor. Venture investors still shudder at the impact on their investments of the "dot-bomb" years 2000 and 2001. Research institutions measure the cost of failed software projects in staggering 11-figure dollar amounts *per year* for the United States alone[2]. Systems integrators struggle to provide integrated systems for their clients using the maximum amount of commercial, off-the-shelf (COTS) software, because the most effective way to reduce the cost and risk of an application development project is to avoid writing software altogether[3].

As an example of how far software application development has fallen out of vogue in the commercial world, one Fortune 500 company recently set a ceiling of $100,000 on all application development projects. (In the commercial world, $100,000 is an extraordinarily low figure for application development.) Exceptions required the approval of the CIO and the CEO[4]. A more eloquent testimony to the extent of the perceived risk would be hard to find.

So what has gone wrong? We have five decades of high-level language development under our belt, the reusability advances of object-oriented software, development methodologies galore, componentized applications, iterative design techniques, massively sophisticated integrated development environments, and, thanks to exponentially increasing desktop computer power, faster write-compile-test cycles than ever before. We teach information technology in our schools, we churn out computer science graduates from our universities, and the registered developers of popular programming languages like Java are numbered in the millions[5]. So why can't we write software successfully?

Sociologists and media experts in the late 20th century increasingly focused on the theme of relational and socioeconomic disconnectedness. A popular approach was to juxtapose the ubiquitous connectivity claims of the information age with the rapidly developing sense of discontinuity and alienation felt between the various strata of Western society[6]. While the jury is undoubtedly still out on these claims, the fact is that software development education and practice have become increasingly disconnected, both in language and in values, from those who define the requirements and articulate the needs for that software. Application developers talk in terms of methodologies, classes, and use cases, whereas clients and business owners worry about marketable features, cash flow, and return on investment (ROI). The points of contact between these two worlds are very limited. For example, a recent analysis of 16 books on software architecture and object-oriented design showed that only two included the word "cost" in the index[7].

In business, the disconnect between these two worlds is further evidenced by their views of the IT department. Although IT departments are typically one of the largest cost centers of any enterprise in our present age, we must remind ourselves that only 40 years ago IT departments did not exist. The common perception in accounting circles is that an IT department is a drain on the bottom line, and because IT skills are usually not the core skills or even the context of most businesses, it's no small wonder that the trend in the 1990s was to outsource them whenever possible.

As Barry Boehm so astutely puts it, the truly enlightened view is that software development is not a cost that should be contained through outsourcing but a "value creation activity." Unfortunately, software engineers are usually not involved in or often do not understand enterprise-level value creation objectives[7].

The boutique New Zealand software development house Green Door Services puts it succinctly when it says, "Software development is easy, but listening and understanding are hard"[8].

There's a Method to the Madness

Software development and software engineering process have not been without methodological support. Indeed, few if any developers working in the field of object-oriented programming would be unaware of methodologies such as the rational unified process (RUP) or eXtreme programming (XP). Others include feature-driven development (FDD) from Peter Coad, and Sun Microsystems' SunTone Architecture Methodology (SunTone AM). It may, therefore, seem rather bold to present what is in effect yet another methodology within a space already so crowded.

However, this book does not seek to present a new methodology; rather this book builds on the groundwork already achieved through the creation of iterative development methodologies. It introduces processes and guidelines geared toward the recognition of software development as a value creation process, governed primarily by cost and investment constraints, for which the overriding objective is the removal or mitigation of financial risk. This is a truly holistic approach in which the needs of the customer are as important as the needs of the developer and in which the customer participates as fully as the developer. This approach of setting iterative development in the context of value creation, is the focus of the book.

If History Teaches Us Anything . . .

The last few years have seen intense scrutiny of the seriously flawed business propositions underlying the dot.com bubble of the late 1990s. At the time, investors and software developers paid little attention to conventional

ROI thinking. The prevailing attitude was that investment in software repaid its investors through the increased capital value of the company on the market *in expectation* of future sales and profits, rather than through more robust metrics like earnings per share.

You'd be forgiven for thinking that traditional ROI thinking had now returned with a vengeance. However, this is not the case. Rather, the very concept of traditional ROI itself is under scrutiny. Many organizations are now unwilling to tolerate ROIs of more than a year. This is astonishing considering that a three- to five-year ROI was the norm in the era preceding the dot.com boom.

Is this a case of throwing the baby out with the bathwater? Perhaps. But this mentality, as long as it persists, presents some unique problems for software developers and organizations that provide software development services. Only very rarely is it possible to return the investment on a major software development project in less than a year. So if short ROIs are the only acceptable ROIs, and software development typically requires longer ROIs, how can software development be funded in the post-dot-bomb era? How is it possible to release the capital necessary to do major software development projects and still have the developer and the investor make money?

The answer lies in a re-evaluation of the traditional ROI model for software and in the rationale behind recent developments in software design methodology.

Methodological approaches to software development have changed significantly in both substance and approach over the past 10 years or so. The revolution in thinking has become so widespread that the idea of developing software from a massive and detailed functional specification, through the creation of a set of carefully coordinated pieces that are subsequently assembled, integrated, and tested, has largely been abandoned. There are many reasons for this.

The problem with the "waterfall" approach, as it is colloquially known, is that it fails to take account of the business reality that the functional specification is rarely complete at the time the development work starts. However, even if it were possible to start with a complete functional specification, human nature being what it is and the constantly changing demands of the market being what they are, midcourse corrections are inevitable. Of course, longer software development cycles result in an increasing number of changes in requirements.

Such single-flow approaches to development have been replaced with methodologies that allow for iterative or phased definitions of requirements, and that are characterized by iterative development cycles. Within this broad church of thinking, many specific and detailed methodologies have emerged, competing with each other in some aspects while complementing each other in other respects. They hold in common the principle that software development is fundamentally an iterative process that needs to be managed and measured as such.

In many respects, iterative methodologies have been successful, and they've certainly captured the attention of academics and practitioners over the past decade. Studies have been performed to demonstrate the effectiveness of iterative approaches[9], tools have been developed to support such methodologies[10], and a new vocabulary has evolved to articulate the concepts inherent in iterative approaches. For example, software is defined in terms of "components," the behaviors of which are defined by "use cases."

The initiative has, however, been largely technically based and primarily justified from technical considerations. While it is widely accepted that software development should be measured and managed on an iterative basis, little attention has been given to the question of how software development should be funded. As we'll see shortly, it's also necessary to define components within this new financial perspective. These financial components play a very different role from that of software components and represent units of marketable value rather than classes or use cases or patterns.

Minimum Marketable Feature

We've spoken earlier about the idea of software development as a value creation activity. In this section we give components of value the ability to be referenced and posit the existence of minimum marketable features (MMFs). MMFs are units of software value creation. They represent components of intrinsic marketable value.

It should not be surprising that a software application can be deconstructed into units of marketable value. Ultimately, commercial software is a product, and purchasers perceive products to have value in many different ways. Typically the value is not perceivable as a monolithic whole, but as a series of features. Simple products may have only one or two features (a hand tool, or an item of clothing for example), but complex products, such as an automobile, can have a whole slew of identifiable, and sometimes optional, features.

What is particularly unique about software products is that the features are often, or even usually, separately deliverable. In other words, a complex software application can have value to a user even if it is incomplete. Indeed, it is often claimed that software is by its very nature always incomplete!

By carefully choosing the way in which software components are assembled, we can create identified units of marketable value well before the application is anywhere near completion. For example, a complex banking application that in its earliest form merely allows the account holder to check a balance online already has some tangible value. However, this concept is rarely true of nonsoftware products. An automobile that consists of only an engine and a wheelbase is unlikely to be thought particularly valuable by the average consumer!

Typically an MMF creates market value in one or more of the following ways:

- Competitive differentiation
- Revenue generation
- Cost saving
- Brand projection
- Enhanced loyalty

Clearly, not all software features are MMFs. For example, referring again to the hypothetical banking application mentioned earlier, a facility to resize the display screen is not an MMF, since it does not meet any of the criteria listed above.

This means that if software is to be built to optimize value creation, it's important to identify and select MMFs very carefully.

MMF Selection

A central tenet of this work is that the MMFs should determine the iterations of the design and development process. In contrast, the iterations in traditional RUP are determined by use-case considerations. In XP the mini-iterations are driven by a subjective selection of user stories, and constrained by technical features and the need to constantly perform integration testing. The approach taken in this book is not so much to attempt to replace RUP or XP, but to complement these methodologies with a degree of financial rigor.

MMF selection and ordering is one of the most important steps in the business of software development. In fact, our approach dedicates substantial analysis to the processes that define, select, and order MMFs.

There are a number of important reasons for this.

1. If units of marketable value exist within a software application, the value creation process needs to recognize and articulate them.
2. Seeing software development as the assembly of units of value creation allows for funding to be made more granular and more closely aligned to iterative delivery. This gives rise to the concept of iterative funding, defined more fully in a later section.
3. If MMFs can be identified and quantified, it is possible to define mechanisms for optimal value creation per unit time and thereby drive the iterative software development process from financial considerations. One possible optimization is to order the creation of MMFs so as to create the maximum value as early as possible. Defining the optimal ordering of MMFs is a critical part of this and is addressed more fully in Chapter 5.
4. By careful ordering (or "sequencing") of MMFs, we may be able to generate mini-ROIs that align with and complement more granular funding. This means a software development project can be ordered in terms of its MMFs, so it becomes self-funding—an optimal but not necessarily always achievable state. Determining whether a development project can become self-funding requires a risk and time analysis. This is also explored more fully later on.

Opening the Black Box of Software Development

Too often software development projects are simply handed to an IT department or to an outside software house by customers who have little understanding of the process of creating software, and for whom the operation has the characteristics of a magic spell. Raw materials are fed in at one end, and a shiny new application eventually pops out the other end.

Sadly this lack of involvement by the customer in the process of software engineering is a weakness of conventional methodologies, where the artisans of software creation exercise their techniques and methodologies in a closed world, making their creations visible only when a release is called for. Studies have shown that this lack of involvement by the business process owners is the main reason so many software development projects fail[2].

We're not suggesting that a customer or venture investor should be involved in the nitty-gritty production of every component of the software. However, one area in which the principles in this book are characteristically and refreshingly different from other methodologies is in their determination to involve the customer and other business stakeholders throughout the software engineering process.

In this respect the incremental funding methodology (IFM) is similar to XP, except that while XP stresses the need for mini-iterations and constant integration testing against a suite of tests that capture the customer's requirements, we involve the customer for financial and spend-control purposes as well as for requirements cross-checking. It is the concept of the MMF that permits this to happen. Through a granular funding model and a series of mini-ROIs, the customer is constantly informed about the financial details of the project's progress and can, together with the developer, identify financial risk earlier and take steps to correct it.

The benefit to the software developer is also significant. The application development work is not only regularly checked against functional requirements, but also regularly checked from a financial standpoint.

As we'll see in later sections, once the developer builds a comprehensive MMF model, cost or time overruns in the construction of a particular MMF may automatically invoke a reordering of other MMFs so as to sustain the maximum value creation per unit time or to preserve the self-funding status of the project.

Risk Control

Risk is usually the foremost consideration in deciding whether to embark on a software development project. For those organizations brave enough to venture into the world of software development, the analysis, measurement, and tracking of risk occupies a substantial share of the effort expended throughout the project lifecycle.

While many methodologies pay lip service to the need to monitor risk, there is little in the way of programmatic or numerical assessment of risk offered in methodologies such as XP or RUP. Usually, risk is treated as a subjective and largely immeasurable quality, whose impact on project or development decisions is generally seen in terms of cost contingency or increased estimates of project development time.

However, in an environment in which both funding and expenditure are measured and controlled in a granular way through the rigorous analysis of MMFs, risk can be factored into cost return or ROI calculations.

Within this scenario, MMFs can be analyzed using techniques that take risk into account in a formal mathematical model.

We adopt this approach, with two major benefits in mind.

- First, through the creation of an initial MMF model with time and risk factors incorporated, it's possible to make well-informed decisions about whether to undertake the project at all. The model allows a development organization to formalize its risk assessment and link this programmatically to price quotations and contingencies.

- Second, because the MMF model is maintained throughout the life-cycle of the project, the risk factors and mini-ROIs are constantly recomputed. This provides a formalized mechanism for making decisions such as whether to incorporate a new feature earlier than intended, or whether to drop a planned feature from the development because of enhanced risk concerns.

Clearly, in both respects, the calculations can be complex for large projects with multiple MMFs. This book assists the developer, project manager, and funding sponsor by providing a detailed guide to constructing MMF models and for sequencing projects for optimum ROI.

Sigma Techniques

The constant assessment and reassessment of the software development life-cycle is a result of our adoption of the Six Sigma Approach[10].

The Six Sigma Approach was originally developed by Motorola as a way to enhance and monitor quality in production processes. Six Sigma is a broad, comprehensive system for building and sustaining business performance, success, and leadership[10]. It was used and enhanced by GE in the 1990s, and has since been adopted in a modified form by information technology companies such as Sun Microsystems with their Sun Sigma program[10].

Through the MMF model and its rigorous calculation and reassessment of risk, return, and benefits, we apply Six Sigma concepts to software development as follows.

Measurable Customer Requirements

We formalize all customer requirements as MMFs, capturing them not only in functional terms through conventional use-case analysis, but also in business terms through the definition and subsequent analysis of risk, reward, and time to market.

Data-Backed Decision Making

We use the quantified risk and time modeling techniques implicit in the treatment of MMFs to determine the sequence of feature construction with the goal of maximum creation of value per unit time in the software development process.

Incorporating the Voice of the Customer

We involve the customer in all the key decisions of software development by providing MMF visibility and through the delivery of a more granular ROI model. This allows a customer or venture investor to track the effectiveness of investment well in advance of the production of the first release of the software and to inject changes in priority or direction that automatically cause the recomputation of the value generation sequence.

Challenging the Status Quo

Continuously reassessing the MMF model as individual features are constructed and mini-ROIs are realized creates an environment in which the feature creation sequence is constantly reassessed. This is in sharp contrast to a software development project driven by a static project plan. This also means that the role of the project manager is a more demanding one, and that the status quo has a lifecycle measured in days or hours rather than weeks. In this respect, the method captures many of the desirable agility traits needed in today's fast-paced, Web-based environment.

Span Organizational Structures

One of the most success-inhibiting aspects of conventional methodologies is their failure to break the black box of software development. By preserving the separation between business and IT, between the marketing organization and the development organization, these methodologies create the potential for miscommunication and for territorially driven behavior, thus enabling developers and architects to operate in a world largely unchallenged by the realities of the marketplace.

In contrast, our approach exposes the ROI model to the developer in detail. At the same time all stakeholders, including marketers, business owners, and venture investors, can see the software development process in their own terms. Such an approach deliberately breaks the software development black box and spans the typical organizational divisions.

Continuously Measurable Progress

Six Sigma is about progress toward perfection, not perfection itself[10]. Recognizing that Six Sigma quality is appropriate in some cases but not in others, the Six Sigma Approach allows quality and completion parameters to be constantly reassessed. For this to occur, there must be continuously measurable progress toward a goal.

The fact that completion is a largely unobtainable goal in software development is widely recognized, and in this respect Six Sigma's pragmatism is well suited to application software development. However, traditional approaches fail to provide the required continuously measurable progress. Instead, software development appears to all but the developers and a few select stakeholders to be a quantum process in which features appear instantaneously and in bursts with each new release of the software. Progress between releases can only be gauged by monitoring the constant reassessment of the estimated date of the next release.

In contrast, IFM, through its more granular MMF model, allows progress to be measured and quantified on a per-feature basis, with genuinely continuous progress measurement.

Summary

This work introduces an approach to software development that is complementary to iterative development methodologies and is characterized by

- the recognition of software development as a value creation exercise;
- the linking of iterative development to iterative funding;
- constant customer involvement in the development process;

- formal models for assessing return on investment throughout the life-cycle;

- the place of primacy given to minimum marketable features (MMFs) in sequencing value creation;

- the breaking of the traditional software development black box; and

- the adoption of Sigma principles for quality.

References

1. Rational Software Corp., "Build Better Software with Rational Suite DevelopmentStudio," published white paper, 2000. Available online at: http://www.rational.com/products/dstudio/whitepapers.jsp

2. The Standish Group, *Chaos Report,* 1995. Available online at: http://www.standishgroup.com/visitor/chaos.htm

3. IBM Software Advisor, December 10, 2002. Available online at: http://ibmsoftwareadvisor.com/doc/11571

4. *CIO Magazine*, "Application Development," Jul. 2001. Available online at: http://www.cio.com/archive/070101/secret.html

5. "Sun Microsystems wants to increase the number of Java developers from 3 million today to as many as 10 million." Taken from the article, "Sun Seeks to Grow Java Developer Base to 10 Million," by Paul Krill and Tom Sullivan, *InfoWorld*, May 21, 2003. Available online at: http://www.infoworld.com/article/03/05/21/HNsunjavaone_1.html

6. Joseph Straubhaar and Robert LaRose, *Media Now: Communications Media in the Information Society,* 2nd ed., Pacific Grove, California: Wadsworth Publishing, 1997.

7. B. Boehm and K. J. Sullivan, "Software Economics: A Roadmap," invited paper, pp. 937–946, 22nd International Conference on Software Engineering, June, 2000.

8. Taken from the Green Doors Services' value statement available online at its Web site: http://www.greendoorservices.com/values.htm

9. Neuman Pande and George Cavanagh, *The Six Sigma Way*, New York: McGraw-Hill, 2000.

10. "The Sun Sigma advantage," Sun Microsystems Featured Stories, 2002. Available online at: http://www.sun.com/2002-0723/feature/index.html

The New ROI

If software development is to be treated as a value creation exercise, a solid understanding of the financial metrics used to evaluate and track value creation activities is necessary. In this chapter we define these metrics and show how they are impacted by the introduction of MMFs and incremental delivery concepts.■

Applications and ROIs

In the world of commercial application software development, good ideas, technology, and design are rarely sufficient to elicit approval for a project. The reality of the commercial world is that software development is an investment. As with any investment, it involves certain risks and is made with the objective of achieving a return on that investment.

Of course, the return on that investment does not have to be in quantifiable financial terms. But usually, unless there is a measurable financial benefit, it is hard to justify an application software development activity, and especially hard to obtain approval from a finance department for that activity. Troy Zierden, business-intelligence capability manager at electronics retailer Best Buy, says it's very difficult to get project approval when returns on investment are intangible, since there's a team of accountants at his company who watch the numbers very closely[1].

Today's software methodologies tend to begin at the point where the development project has been approved, that is, after the ROI discussions have taken place and conventional methods of measuring ROI have been applied. The software designer, or the software methodologist, is usually not involved in the ROI discussions. As a result, the reasons for funding a project are largely opaque to the designer. Sadly, this means that the designer rarely has any input on the ROI discussions. Our approach changes this, by breaking the black box of application software development, and engaging architects and designers in the investment that we call software development. The result is a radical transformation of the traditional ROI model.

Why ROIs Matter

Let's imagine that you, or your client, want to construct an electronic bill payment system for a retail bank. You estimate that it will permit customers to pay bills two to three times faster than via an ATM and ten times faster than standing in line to present a check payment to a bank teller. You intuitively know that this system will make your customers happy and more loyal to the bank. You're excited about writing it and you can certainly justify why you should do so in terms of customer loyalty and ease-of-use benefits.

Unfortunately, none of these reasons or motivations will cut it with the finance department! Although the benefits sound interesting, and perhaps even compelling, they are not in a measurable form. What the finance people are looking for is a number, a dollar figure, to which those benefits translate for the company's bottom line. Finding that figure isn't as easy as it might seem. But it may be one of the most important decisions to be made in the lifecycle of this software development project; one so crucial that it could actually halt the project completely or cause it to be stillborn. This is neither the time nor the place for the developer to fade into the background. It's often here that the success or failure of an application software development project is ultimately determined. And it's not as though financial approval is going away or becoming less important. Over 80% of IT managers surveyed in 2001 reported that the importance of ROI has increased compared to the previous year[2].

Dataquest reports that in these "trying times . . . IT investments are being looked into more closely than ever before." They suggest that the best strategy involves finding a business sponsor to back the investments, and that without this type of sponsorship it becomes very difficult to justify the costs of implementing the project[3].

The Business Case

Ultimately the calculation of ROI compares the financial impact of different options over time. The time context is essential. Without it, an ROI is meaningless. Typically it starts with a question of the form,

"Should we spend $1,000,000 to develop part of the system over two years or $1,500,000 to develop all of the system over three years?"

The answer to a question such as this emerges from the construction of a business case. A business case is best described as a financial story based on facts, structured assumptions, and logic. It provides a vehicle by which the financial impact of the options can be examined and conclusions drawn.

Cash Flow Projections

At the heart of a business case is a cash flow projection. It is a sequence of calculations of a specific financial position over time. To construct a cash flow projection, we need to look at the net financial situation at each of the time intervals. Cash flow projections are typically calculated on a monthly basis, though for longer projects they may be calculated quarterly. The key thing about cash flow projections is that for each calculation point, all the costs and all the benefits have to be factored in as they occur.

Let's look at an example. Imagine that we're considering an application development project to create a customer relationship management (CRM) system that is intended ultimately to eliminate a call center. How do we quantify the impact in cash flow terms?

Clearly the major benefit is the removal of the costs associated with the call center. But for a cash flow analysis we need to know when those costs are taken out of the equation. It's also important to understand what the components of the savings are. There are, for example, the operational costs of the center, the possible capital gain from the sales of the land, buildings, or lease, and perhaps other savings associated with facilities management.

On the benefits side, we need to quantify factors such as the increased customer satisfaction created as a result of a more responsive CRM experience. Other factors include the additional revenue achieved by attracting new customers because of our reputation for processing customer calls faster.

In the cash flow analysis, these positive and negative factors are computed for each period in the analysis. By summing these factors, we can determine whether the project is cash-positive or cash-negative over its development lifecycle.

Payback Time

The lifecycle cash position isn't the only information we can derive from a cash flow analysis. A cash flow picture also indicates the extent to which the business is investing in the project at each period in the analysis. It quantifies the "investment flow" if you will. Normally, as a project starts to return revenue, this investment flow is reduced and will likely become zero prior to the end of the project. At this point the project is said to have become "self-funding" or to have reached "self-funding status." It no longer needs cash injections from the business to sustain it.

This does not mean the project has reached a breakeven point, however, as there may still be a debt to repay to the business (see discussion of breakeven time below). We will call the period between self-funding status and breakeven status the "repayback period." Figure 2.1 illustrates these points over the timespan of a successful application development project.

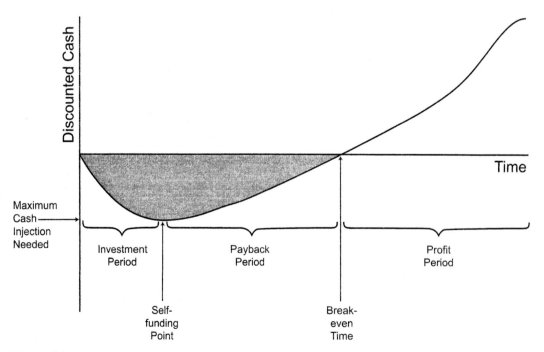

Figure 2.1
A Successful Application Development Project

Present Value of Future Money

To recap, conventional ROI analysis is about measuring the amount of the payback and the time in which is it achieved.

For example, a project that becomes profitable in 18 months is intuitively more compelling than a project that takes five years to become profitable. However, it may not be financially more compelling over the long term. It's possible that the return from the five-year project is significantly larger than the one from the 18-month project. Under these circumstances, how is it possible to decide if the five-year project is to be preferred over the 18-month project?

Clearly money has a time value. A piece of software that delivers $1 million in savings in one year is more interesting than a piece of software that delivers $1 million in savings in 20 years. So how do we compare the value of $1 million next year with $1 million in 20 years?

To some extent the value of future cash can be measured by discounting it against an assumed interest rate. This calculates the present value (PV) of the future cash. This approach is clearly simplistic because it fails to take into account risk factors associated with the predicted future cash, but more on this later. For now, we'll assume the future cash is certain. As an illustration, imagine that the interest rate is i%. The present value of x in n years' time is defined as follows:

$$PV = \$x \ / \ (1 + i/100)^n$$

In other words, if we assume an interest rate of 5% per year, receiving $1 million in 20 years is equivalent to gaining $1/(1 + 0.05)^{20}$ = approximately $377,000 now. On the other hand, receiving $1 million next year is equivalent to gaining approximately $952,000 now.

Net Present Value

We can create an overall figure for the net cash position of the project by calculating the cash position for each time period in the development cycle (month, quarters, or years) and then summing the PV corrections. The set of PV-corrected cash positions is known as the discounted cash flow (DCF). The sum of these positions is known as the net present value (NPV). An example of an NPV calculation is given shortly.

Because the NPV allows us to measure the overall value of the software development, even if its returns are spread over a period of time, DCF tends to be a more useful measurement of a software development project's projected costs and returns than either net cash or ROI. In general, when we refer to the cash position we'll be implying DCF. It is for this reason that Figure 2.1 reflects DCF rather than just a straight cash flow position. This will become especially important as we look at the effect of iterative software development approaches and the order in which MMFs are executed.

Breakeven Time

An important metric that emerges from a DCF calculation is the "breakeven time," or the point in the lifecycle at which the project reaches "breakeven status." This is the number of periods (e.g., months, quarters, or years) before the return from the new software, corrected for time, matches the costs expended to create it. In other words, it is the point at which the rolling NPV transitions from a negative value to a positive value. A project that has reached breakeven status is making real money for the business. We call this the "profit period." The breakeven time thus marks the end of the *payback period* and the start of the profit period.

Before the dot-bomb era, breakeven times of five years were not atypical. In today's market however, software developments with a breakeven time of more than 12 to 18 months are rarely approved.

Internal Rate of Return

Another factor in conventional ROI analysis is the internal rate of return (IRR). This is the interest rate, or cost of capital, at which the NPV for the project becomes zero.

The usefulness of IRR is a matter of some debate, so it is not a term we deal with extensively in this book. However, it is an interesting concept, for the following reason.

NPV alone does not give us enough information to answer the question "is this project worth doing?" If a particular development project has an NPV greater than zero, undertaking the project is certainly a better investment than doing nothing at all. However, it doesn't tell us anything about whether this is the best thing to be doing in comparison with other possible money-generating activities.

For example, if the application's NPV is positive only when interest rates are 6% per year or less, but we know we can get an 8% return from low-risk bank deposits, the application development may not be worth doing. We would make more money just by depositing the money in a bank. The IRR, or the interest rate at which the NPV is zero, is thus an interesting metric in conventional ROI analysis and provides us with a useful yardstick for evaluating a positive NPV.

Summary of the Terms

Briefly, the terms introduced so far can be summarized as follows:

- Return on investment: The amount of undiscounted cash (profit) returned by the project over the lifecycle, divided by the undiscounted cash (investment) used to fund the project over the lifecycle, expressed as a percentage.
- Self-funding point: The number of time periods until the business no longer needs to inject cash into the project to sustain it.
- Present value: The value of future cash converted to the present time.
- Discounted cash flow: The cash flow with PV corrections applied to each period.
- Net present value: The sum of the DCF.
- Breakeven time: The time until the NPV of the project becomes positive (i.e., the point at which the project is making real money).
- Internal rate of return: The interest rate at which the NPV becomes zero.

Now let's see how this all works in practice.

An Example

In this example project we analyze a software development effort over five one-year periods.

An early release of the software allows revenue to start flowing in year 4, though in practice it's not until year 5 that the real revenue flow starts. On the cost side there are some early capital outlays associated with buying the hardware and software needed to do the development work. A technology refresh cycle in year 4 updates the development hardware and some of the data center facilities. In addition to the capital costs, there are operational costs related to personnel, support, data center facilities fees, and marketing.

In addition some savings arise from using the software internally within the organization. Figure 2.2 captures these figures. The numbers are $US in thousands.

Figure 2.2 shows that we have a five-year project that requires $2,760,000 to fund. The project generates cash in years 4 and 5. After five years, the total cash returned is $1,288,000. This represents a ROI of 1,288,000/2,760,000 = ~47% over five years.

We now turn to the PV analysis to examine the NPV of the project. The table in Figure 2.3 shows the calculations for three annual discount rates: 5%, 10%, and (for reasons that will be clear in a moment) 12.8%. We have used the standard NPV convention of assuming the cash is generated, or the cost incurred, at the end of each period. Values have been rounded to the nearest integer.

The discount rate at which the NPV is zero turns out to be 12.8%. By reference to Figures 2.2 and 2.3, we can draw the following conclusions about this application development project:

Description			Periods					Total
			1	2	3	4	5	
Income								
	Revenue					1,000	3,800	**4,800**
	Savings					200	600	**800**
Total Income			0	0	0	1,200	4,400	**5,600**
Expenditure								
	Capital							
		Hardware	700	20	20	200	20	**960**
		Software	300					**300**
	Total Capital		1,000	20	20	200	20	**1,260**
	Operating							
		Headcount	240	360	550	360	112	**1,622**
		Data Center	30	30	30	30	30	**150**
		Support	140	120	120	150	150	**680**
		Marketing	0	0	100	200	300	**600**
	Total Operating		410	510	800	740	592	**3,052**
Total Expenditure			1,410	530	820	940	612	**4,312**
Cash			-1,410	-530	-820	260	3,788	**1,288**
Investment			-1,410	-530	-820			**-2,760**
ROI								**47%**

Figure 2.2
Classic ROI Analysis ($US in Thousands)

Period		1	2	3	4	5	
Cash		-1,410	-530	-820	260	3,788	
Self-funding Status					X		
							NPV
DCF @	5.0%	-1,343	-481	-708	214	2,968	650
	Rolling NPV	-1,343	-1,824	-2,532	-2,318	650	
	Breakeven Status					X	
	10.0%	-1,282	-438	-616	178	2,352	194
	Rolling NPV	-1,282	-1,720	-2,336	-2,158	194	
	Breakeven Status					X	
	12.8%	-1,251	-417	-572	161	2,079	0
	Rolling NPV	-1,251	-1,667	-2,239	-2,079	0	

Figure 2.3
NPV Analysis ($US in Thousands)

- The project generates $5.6 million over five years, at a total cost of $4.3 million.
- The business invests a total of $2.76 million at various points over that period to fund it.
- The project pays back that investment and returns an additional $1.288 million to the business after five years.
- The resulting ROI over that period is 47%.
- The project reaches self-funding status in year 4.
- Breakeven status is achieved somewhere in year 5.
- The NPV of the project, assuming an annual discount rate of 5%, is $650,000.
- The NPV of the project, assuming an annual discount rate of 10%, is $194,000.
- The IRR of the project is 12.8%.

Despite the apparent attractiveness of the ROI, the IRR indicates that it's only worth undertaking this development project if we're unable to find other uses of investment capital yielding better than 12.8% over five years.

If the project is perceived to be risky, this rate of return is probably insufficient to persuade a CIO to proceed. An alternative but lower-risk use of the money with just (say) a 10% rate of return may be thought more attractive.

The bottom line is that at this IRR and in today's market, the project will probably not get approved.

Incorporating MMFs into the Financial Case

Now let's take a look at that funding model again. As it stands currently, it's a classic ROI scenario in which we invest the majority of the capital up front and achieve a return only at the very end of the lifecycle. Intuitively, this is unsurprising. The application clearly has to be designed, written, integrated, tested, and packaged before sales of the software result in a revenue flow to offset the development costs.

But suppose it were possible to generate revenue earlier? How would this impact the ROI model?

At first, these may seem like theoretical questions. After all, how can revenue be released before the development work has been completed?

However, imagine we were able to separate the application into groups of features that, although they represented just a subset of the overall application feature set, were still inherently marketable. These MMFs would by definition be capable of creating revenue when released independently and incrementally.

We explore the concept of an MMF and discuss how use cases or user stories can be composed into an MMF in Chapter 3.

For now, let's assume that the total functionality of this application can be partitioned into four distinct MMFs. We'll imagine that we can develop the MMFs sequentially, aiming to bring one to market each year in years 2, 3, 4, and 5 of the project. For the purposes of this example we'll assume each MMF is equally valuable.

In year 2 we get a small revenue flow from MMF 1. In year 3 we get revenue from MMFs 1 and 2, and so on.

There are clearly additional costs associated with packaging and releasing these early MMFs, so this needs to be taken into account in the financial model. There are also additional headcount costs, because of the additional testing at the MMF level.

Taking these into account, and again using broad-brush estimates only, the returns of our modified project are shown in Figure 2.4.

The PV analysis, using the same conventions as previously, reveals the modified NPV of the project as shown in Figure 2.5.

The incremental delivery approach produces a development project that now looks like this:

- The project generates $7.8 million (vs. $5.6 million) over five years, at a total cost of $4.712 million.

Description			Periods					Total
			1	2	3	4	5	
Income								
	Revenue			700	1,400	2,100	2,800	**7,000**
	Savings						200	600	**800**
Total Income			0	700	1,400	2,300	3,400	**7,800**
Expenditure								
	Capital							
		Hardware	700	20	20	200	20	**960**
		Software	300					**300**
	Total Capital		1,000	20	20	200	20	**1,260**
	Operating							
		Headcount	240	360	550	360	112	**1,622**
		Data Center	30	30	30	30	30	**150**
		Support	140	120	120	150	150	**680**
		Marketing	200	200	200	200	200	**1,000**
	Total Operating		610	710	900	740	492	**3,452**
Total Expenditure			1,610	730	920	940	512	**4,712**
Cash			-1,610	-30	480	1,360	2,888	**3,088**
Investment			-1,610	-30				**-1,640**
ROI								**188%**

Figure 2.4
ROI Analysis Using MMFs ($US in Thousands)

Period		1	2	3	4	5	
Cash		-1,610	-30	480	1,360	2,888	
Self-funding Status				X			
							NPV
DCF @	5.0%	-1,533	-27	415	1,119	2,263	**2,236**
	Rolling NPV	-1,533	-1,561	-1,146	-27	2,236	
	Breakeven Status				X		
	10.0%	-1,464	-25	361	929	1,793	**1,594**
	Rolling NPV	-1,464	-1,488	-1,128	-199	1,594	
	Breakeven Status				X		
	36.3%	-1,181	-16	190	394	614	**0**
	Rolling NPV	-1,181	-1,197	-1,008	-614	0	

Figure 2.5
NPV Analysis Using MMFs ($US in Thousands)

- The business invests a total of $1.64 million to fund it (vs. $2.76 million).
- The project returns that investment and pays back an additional $3.088 million at the end of five years.
- The resulting ROI over that period is 188% (vs. 47%).

- The project reaches self-funding status in year 3 (vs. year 4).
- Breakeven status is achieved during year 5.
- The NPV of the project, assuming an annual discount rate of 5%, is $2.236 million (vs. $650,000).
- The NPV of the project, assuming an annual discount rate of 10%, is $1.594 million (vs. $194,000).
- The IRR of the project is 36.3%.

Comparing the MMF-based ROI with the Classic ROI

Clearly, the impact of using incremental delivery of MMFs in this example transforms the project. It costs just a little more to undertake the project, but the impact in terms of overall revenue, five-year ROI, and the IRR is attractive. The revenue over five years is higher primarily because it starts earlier. However, for the purposes of this simplified analysis we have assumed nothing about changes in marketability over the five years. With an IRR of ~36%, this now appears to be an excellent way to deploy the investment capital over five years.

The self-funding time is particularly significant. Now we have a project that is self-sufficient in cash terms as early as year 3. We will expand on this idea of self-funding development projects in later sections.

Taking the Risks into Account

This financial analysis has by necessity been oversimplified. Several variables were not taken into account. One of the most important of these is risk.

In general, incremental delivery has the benefit of reducing overall project risk. But for this to be both demonstrated and measurable, it's necessary to implement a mechanism for taking risk into account in an MMF context.

The quantification of risk has an immediate impact on the perceived value of an MMF and must therefore be factored into the financial equations. We may decide, for example that an MMF yielding $1 million in two years' time at 90% risk is less valuable than one yielding $500,000 in two years' time at 10% risk. Of course, this raises the important question of what is meant by 90% risk and 10% risk.

There are many approaches to handling risk assessment in complex projects, and in fact much has already been written on the topic. The approach that we adopt is more fully explored in Chapter 3.

The Impact of MMF Ordering

In the previous simplified example, there were only a few MMFs, and they were easy to identify, were all equally valuable in revenue terms, and all took the same amount of time to develop. In this idealized scenario the question of which MMF to develop first does not arise.

In the real world, things are usually quite different. The task of grouping use cases to create MMFs is to some extent both an art and a methodological process. Furthermore, the order in which MMFs are developed can radically affect the financial model of the project. At the very least, it can determine whether the project is self-funding or not.

This subject is explored in the next chapter.

Summary

- Analysis of the financial context for a software development project requires an understanding of breakeven time, net present value, and internal rate of return.

- Introducing MMFs impacts these financial metrics, usually for the better.

- MMF ordering, MMF risk evaluation, and the parallelization of MMF sequencing all determine the extent to which those financial metrics are impacted.

References

1. Sandra Swanson, "Business Intelligence—Can't Live Without It," *Information Week*, March 13, 2002.

2. Mary Hayes, "Payback Time: Making Sure ROI Measures Up," *Information Week*, August 6, 2001.

3. "It's All About ROI," *Dataquest CIO*, January 10, 2002.

Identifying and Valuing Marketable Features

Agility and time to market are critical for success in today's fast-paced IT environment. A software development project can be optimized for financial performance by defining it in terms of MMFs. In this section we introduce methods for eliciting MMFs and define the incremental funding methodology (IFM).■

Incremental Funding Methodology

In Chapter 2 we introduced the concept that a carefully prioritized delivery schedule optimizes the ROI of a project. If limited funds are available for financing a project, this has the effect of enhancing the project's cash flow so that revenue can be generated earlier to offset the development costs of subsequent MMFs, thereby lowering capital demand.

Usually, the delivery schedule that results in the optimum cash flow is not the same one that optimizes total ROI. As a result, business stakeholders often need to strike a balance between these two goals. For reasons that will become clear shortly, our approach is to optimize for overall ROI while providing detailed cash flow forecasting to support the flexibility needed by the business.

To optimize for ROI, we must identify, define, and validate MMFs that deliver clear value to the organization. MMF value can be described in concrete financial terms ("tangible MMFs") or in less tangible terms ("intangible

MMFs"). In this chapter we explain exactly what we mean by the term "minimum marketable feature," and then describe techniques for eliciting and defining an MMF. Chapter 4 examines our approach to handling the architectural or framework elements that must be present before an MMF can be constructed, and introduces the concept of incremental architecture. Chapters 5 and 6 describe techniques for sequencing and ordering MMFs for maximum effect. In Chapter 7 we revisit the question of intangibles and examine how to evaluate and prioritize MMFs whose benefits may be hard to quantify financially. Collectively, these concepts define what we call the incremental funding methodology (IFM).

IFM is not the only approach that recognizes the importance of delivering market-valued features to the customer. Recently there has been a tremendous surge of interest in agile methodologies, the underlying philosophy of which is that customer-valued software should be delivered early and continuously, and that changing requirements must be welcomed, even late in the process[1,2]. To accomplish this, agile approaches such as XP and SCRUM[3,4] minimize up-front planning and design, and focus instead on shorter plans that deliver customer-valued functionality in small increments. Change is embraced whenever it occurs, and modeling and documentation are minimized in order to allow agile developers to "travel light."

Similarly, IFM values timely and incremental delivery of functionality to the customer, and embraces change as a way of life in the Internet age. However, as we shall see in Chapter 4, IFM also embraces a new concept known as "incremental architecture." This approach provides the benefits of an architectural approach without the disadvantages of the usual up-front costs. The IFM sequencing heuristic enables developers to make informed decisions about how much planning and how much up-front design should be performed. As we shall see in the following chapters, the heuristic is invaluable in complex projects, where examining all possible development sequences is computationally unfeasible in reasonable time.

IFM is a process-neutral methodology that can be applied in a variety of software development processes. In Chapters 8 and 9 we discuss the application of IFM in RUP and agile environments, and show how its use can enhance the delivery process in both cases.

Minimum Marketable Features

As the name implies, an MMF is characterized by the three attributes: minimum, marketable, and feature.

Probably the most significant characteristic of an MMF is the fact that it represents a distinct and deliverable feature of the system. Webster's dictionary describes a feature as "the structure, form, or appearance" of an entity, or as its "prominent characteristic." A feature is therefore something that is observable to the user. For example, in an online travel agency application, a flight planner and an online tour organizer might be seen as distinct features. In contrast, a class library would not be considered a feature because it provides no clear-cut and deliverable functionality to the user. Similarly, an underlying architectural layer that provides the infrastructure for an application would likewise not be a feature, because it only provides value when delivered within the context of the entire application.

An MMF also must provide significant value to the customer. We use the term "marketable" to describe this concept. However, value can be measured in many ways, such as revenue generation, cost savings, competitive differentiation, brand-name projection, and enhanced customer loyalty. Even this list is by no means exclusive, as true value can only be defined within the context of the proposed project and measured by the organization developing the software.

In Chapter 7 we discuss other, less tangible benefits that may create significant value in an MMF even though quantifying them in terms of hard ROI may be extremely difficult.

The general approach taken by IFM is to identify the minimum or smallest possible group of features that deliver significant value to the user. Of course, the meanings of the terms "minimum" and "significant" are debatable and can be interpreted by developers according to the context of their currently adopted development process.

Within a more traditional approach such as RUP[5], a feature might be identified as a system use case or a fairly large module, while in a more agile approach such as feature-driven development (FDD), a feature is defined as a "tiny, granular piece of client-valued function"[6]. However, what we find as we apply IFM within these various paradigms is that the recognizable size of a *marketable* feature tends to stay the same. The difference lies in the extent to which the underlying entities need to be composed in order to form the marketable feature.

The ideal MMF is a small, self-contained feature that can be developed quickly and that delivers significant value to the user. An MMF that requires extensive effort to construct and returns low value to the customer may be identified as an MMF, but it will probably not be prioritized early within the delivery schedule unless it is needed by another, more profitable MMF. Some

MMFs may well be uneconomical to develop at all, a characteristic that is revealed by the IFM heuristic in Chapter 5.

The range and number of potential MMFs in a project can be quite large, and it is usually not immediately apparent how to optimize the development strategy. Through the rigorous definition of MMFs and techniques for prioritization and sequencing, IFM brings clarity to this area of ambiguity.

Candidate MMFs

Candidate MMFs are identified primarily through considering and analyzing the problem to be solved within the context of the application domain, stakeholders' needs and constraints, and the current business context.

MMF elicitation can be either a top-down or a bottom-up activity. In the top-down approach, a high-level problem statement of the system is defined and serves as the starting point for identifying further critical system features. The entire system is initially considered to be a single MMF. It is then analyzed for constituent parts, which are formed into a second layer of MMFs in the decomposition. Each of these MMFs is then analyzed to determine whether it can be broken into smaller features. Figure 3.1 illustrates this process for an online travel agency. Top-down decomposition is very useful for decomposing large systems, whether they are structured or object-oriented in nature. This approach is described in more depth as part of the software decomposition process known as "function-class decomposition"[7,8].

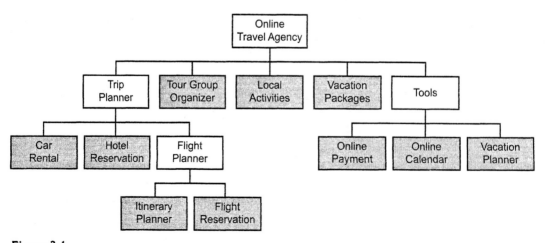

Figure 3.1
Top-down Decomposition of a System into MMFs

In this example, the system level MMF is labeled "Online Travel Agency," and is decomposed into five MMFs at the next level: *trip planner, tour group organizer, local activities, vacation packages,* and *tools.* Each of these is then examined to see whether any further decomposition is possible. Trip planner is decomposed into *car rental, hotel reservation,* and *flight planner,* while *tools* is decomposed into *online payment, online calendar,* and *vacation planner.* One further level of decomposition refines *flight planner* into *itinerary planner* and *flight reservation.*

The actual MMFs are found at the "leaves" of the tree and are shown as shaded nodes in the diagram. Decomposition stops when the leaf nodes cannot be further decomposed into parts that return meaningful value to the customer. Each candidate MMF must then be analyzed to determine the costs and benefits that it brings to the project.

In the bottom-up approach stakeholders identify primitive components of the system and must then compose them into larger units that meet the criterion of an MMF. The following section explains how to identify candidate MMFs and how to evaluate their quality.

Determining the Value of an MMF

To understand the value of an MMF, we need to identify and analyze the value that it will return, and express this as specific projections of revenue and other less quantifiable objectives. The following questions must be asked concerning the projected costs and values for each MMF.

1. **What type of value will this MMF return?** The perceived value of each MMF must be clearly stated and, where possible, translated into terms of projected cash flow over a specified period of time. For example, the significant value of the flight reservation depicted in Figure 3.1 might be defined as follows:

   - **Savings in office personnel costs.** These savings are possible because customers are now empowered to find and book their own flights, therefore reducing the number of office personnel and space needed. The extent of the savings will depend on the number of current customers who use this new option instead of making personal visits to the travel agency.

   - **Increased number of customers.** It is projected that an online presence would increase the exposure of the travel agency and result in a growth in the customer base. This is expected to increase the number of sales, which would lead to a related increase in revenue.

- **Improved customer retention.** Current storefront customers who might otherwise have been drawn to competitors' online sales venues would be retained through the creation of this online service. This benefit results in saving revenue that might have otherwise been lost.

The categorization of these factors as tangible or intangible benefits is a fuzzy one and depends to a large extent on the ability of the organization to quantify the projected returns. A benefit that might be considered intangible to one organization may well be considered tangible to an organization with more advanced market and trend analysis capabilities.

2. **Can that value be translated into a dollar amount?** Usually any commercial software development project is preceded by a degree of market analysis. If this analysis is sufficiently fine grained, it's relatively straightforward to take projected uptake and usage figures, and combine them with development cost estimates to quantify the projected returns for MMFs. Within such a scenario, costs and revenues can be predicted over a series of time periods.

   As an example, the table in Figure 3.2 shows two MMFs, designated A and B, for which costs and expected revenues have been predicted for a project whose success will be measured over 12 months. The figures are in thousands of $US. MMF A takes two periods to develop, whereas MMF B requires just one. However, MMF A returns more revenue than MMF B.

   The ROI from each MMF depends on when in the 12-month project lifecycle the MMF is constructed. For example, if we assume that only one MMF will be developed per period, then we can only start one or the other of these in period 1 of the project, how do we decide whether MMF A's larger development cost but better returns outweighs MMF B's smaller costs but slower returns? We can find the answer to this question by calculating the NPV of the MMF returns, as explained in Chapter 2.

MMF	Cost and Revenue per Period											
	1	2	3	4	5	6	7	8	9	10	11	12
A	-200	-200	100	120	140	160	200	220	240	300	320	340
B	-250	50	50	80	100	120	140	160	180	200	200	200

Figure 3.2
Cost and Revenue for Two Sample MMFs (in $US Thousands)

IFM calculates the NPV of each MMF for each possible starting period during the development phase of the project. The formula for calculating NPV from a vector of costs and returns was presented in Chapter 2. The table in Figure 3.3 shows the calculation for MMF A, assuming a discount rate of 10% per year (0.8% per month). In accordance with the standard conventions, the cost or return is taken at the end of the period.

In IFM these position-dependent NPVs are called "sequence-adjusted net present values" (SANPVs). Figure 3.4 summarizes the SANPVs for our two sample MMFs using a table format that we use throughout the book.

MMF A (Months)												NPV
1	2	3	4	5	6	7	8	9	10	11	12	10%/yr
-200	-200	100	120	140	160	200	220	240	300	320	340	1,604
0	-200	-200	100	120	140	160	200	220	240	300	320	1,285
0	0	-200	-200	100	120	140	160	200	220	240	300	986
0	0	0	-200	-200	100	120	140	160	200	220	240	708
0	0	0	0	-200	-200	100	120	140	160	200	220	486
0	0	0	0	0	-200	-200	100	120	140	160	200	283
0	0	0	0	0	0	-200	-200	100	120	140	160	101
0	0	0	0	0	0	0	-200	-200	100	120	140	-44
0	0	0	0	0	0	0	0	-200	-200	100	120	-170
0	0	0	0	0	0	0	0	0	-200	-200	100	-277
0	0	0	0	0	0	0	0	0	0	-200	-200	-365

MMF A (Months)												NPV
1	2	3	4	5	6	7	8	9	10	11	12	10%/yr
-250	50	50	80	100	120	140	160	180	200	200	200	1,138
0	-250	50	50	80	100	120	140	160	180	200	200	949
0	0	-250	50	50	80	100	120	140	160	180	200	761
0	0	0	-250	50	50	80	100	120	140	160	180	574
0	0	0	0	-250	50	50	80	100	120	140	160	407
0	0	0	0	0	-250	50	50	80	100	120	140	260
0	0	0	0	0	0	-250	50	50	80	100	120	132
0	0	0	0	0	0	0	-250	50	50	80	100	22
0	0	0	0	0	0	0	0	-250	50	50	80	-68
0	0	0	0	0	0	0	0	0	-250	50	50	-140
0	0	0	0	0	0	0	0	0	0	-250	50	-184
											-250	-248

Figure 3.3
NPV for Our Two Sample MMFs According to Start Period (in $US Thousands)

MMF	Period											
	1	2	3	4	5	6	7	8	9	10	11	12
A	1604	1285	986	708	486	283	101	-44	-170	-277	-365	N/A
B	1138	949	761	574	407	260	132	22	-68	-140	-184	-248

Figure 3.4
SANPVs for Our Two Sample MMFs (in $US Thousands)

The SANPV figures provide valuable information about the merits of constructing a particular MMF at different points in the project. For example, MMF A must be implemented sometime in the first seven periods if it is to be profitable, whereas MMF B could be started as late as period 8 and still make money.

In addition, the SANPVs reveal the relative benefits of different MMFs if we're making a choice about which to implement. For example, in period 1 MMF A is the better choice because it has an NPV of $1.6 million, versus only $1.1 million for MMF B. But in period 7, MMF B would be a better choice, with its NPV of $132,000, versus only $101,000 for MMF A.

Clearly, if IFM is to optimize project sequencing for maximum ROI, each MMF must be carefully analyzed in terms of these SANPVs.

3. **How can intangible benefits be justified?** The value of a software application cannot simply be measured in terms of standard ROI. To do so would minimize the importance of other intangible factors that are widely recognized to contribute value to an IT project. These intangibles include values that are difficult to quantify in terms of a dollar amount, but which will return some sort of value to the organization. The difficulty is often in quantifying exactly what that value is. As an example, consider the assumption that a certain IT project would result in "happier customers" or "improved business knowledge." The intuitive belief is that benefits will follow. The difficulties emerge when we try to quantify the extent of this payback.

   In a recent study conducted by *InformationWeek*[9], 200 IT and business professionals were asked how they weighed the benefits of intangibles versus standard ROI when determining how to invest IT dollars. Forty-seven percent reported that they weighed them equally, 33% reported that ROI measurements were more important than intangible assumptions, and 20% reported that intangibles were weighed more heavily than ROI measurements. Clearly, many businesses and organizations value the role of intangible assumptions in the decision-making process.

The approach taken by IFM is that both tangible and intangible benefits should be considered when assessing MMFs. Making all decisions based solely on traditional ROI methods risks failing to take into consideration many other organizational values that may lead in less tangible ways to the future growth and health of the company. At the same time, decisions based on intangible assumptions should be backed up with solid calculations that clearly show the cost of the decision in terms of lost opportunities for generating more predictable cash flows. IFM can therefore be categorized as an ROI-informed, rather than an ROI-driven approach.

With this in mind, we must recognize an MMF as a piece of deliverable functionality, valued in terms of both quantifiable income generation potential and less tangible benefits. Chapter 7 deals with how we value the intangible aspects of an MMF.

4. **What are the risk factors associated with this MMF?** Risk factors must be considered when developing a software application. An MMF with an ROI of $500,000 over two years might look extremely interesting to the developers, but if there is only a 30% likelihood of its successful development and delivery, then the perceived value of the MMF to the business would decrease and might be considered less attractive than, for example, an MMF with an ROI of $200,000 over two years for which the perceived risk is negligible.

   Clearly, a full risk analysis needs be conducted for each MMF in which the probability and impact of each identified risk is quantified[10]. Risks can then be listed in order of severity. Usually, individual risks are calculated as

   % risk value = % probability of risk × % impact severity of risk

   In general, risks modify the figures in the MMF vector.

   Certain types of risks are highly correlated to the delivery schedule, and because IFM is particularly concerned with this schedule, these risks are of particular interest. For example, the risk of a competitor's product hitting the market first and getting the lion's share of potential customers is a significant one that can be mitigated if it is possible to guarantee early delivery.

   MMF risk assessment therefore needs to distinguish between risks related to development costs and risks related to project revenues that are primarily outside the control of the project team. For IFM purposes, we assume the application of normal software engineering practices that identify and mitigate development-related risks. The assumption is that the development costs plugged into the IFM model already reflect these risks.

Similarly, revenue-related risks need to be considered and reflected in the returns portion of the MMF vector. For example, if an MMF exhibited a certain revenue-related risk with a probability of 5% and a severity of 7%, and a second risk at a probability of 10% and severity of 10%, this would give rise to a total risk multiplier of $(0.05 \times 0.07) + (0.1 \times 0.1) = 0.0135$. For a single-period revenue projected at \$20,000, the equivalent risk factor for that period would be calculated as \$20,000 $\times$ 0.0135 = \$270, and the revenue for the period would be reduced to \$19,730.

Clearly, a variety of approaches exist for recognizing and computing risk in any investment process. IFM takes a strictly neutral view on the mechanism for applying risk to the MMF numbers. However, for IFM to work successfully, it is essential that a risk analysis be performed so that the risks are factored into the MMF costs and returns.

5. **What cost and effort is required to develop this MMF?** IFM requires an analysis of the time and effort required to develop an MMF and a translation of that effort into development costs. A detailed description of how to accomplish this is beyond the scope of this book and has been described in detail in other publications. Typical approaches involve predicting the size and complexity of the product to be developed, and translating those metrics into effort and cost requirements. One of the most popular approaches is Barry Boehm's constructive cost model (COCOMO)[11,12]. This process requires the developer to estimate the size of the application either in lines of code (LOC) or in function points. Effort and resource requirements are calculated by answering a series of questions about project characteristics and applying a series of formulas. This approach could be viewed as a top-down method for project estimation.

   Another popular method uses a bottom-up approach in which a finely detailed work-breakdown structure (WBS) is developed[13]. The cost of the lowest-level tasks is then estimated, and the individual lower-level estimates are summed to produce the total cost and effort estimates. The assumption is that errors in lower-level estimates will cancel each other out to produce a fairly realistic estimate.

   Effective methods for bridging the gap between MMF definition and cost estimation depend somewhat on the size and nature of the MMF. IFM deliberately does not specify any particular estimation technique and assumes that the method used is customary for the project team.

For example, in an agile environment where developers estimate the development effort required for each user story, the total effort of an MMF can be obtained by summing the effort of all its component user stories. In other, more traditional environments a more formal estimation method such as COCOMO or a WBS should be used.

6. **What is the anticipated time duration needed to develop this MMF?**
The required effort must then be translated into a duration estimate. Of course this depends to some extent on the staff available for development. At this early stage of MMF definition and validation, a reasonable manpower assignment that reflects anticipated personnel availability is used to determine the anticipated duration of the MMF development period.

Development and Delivery Precursors

Ultimately, it is the SANPV values of the MMF that determine whether its development can be justified. MMFs with a negative SANPV are clearly unattractive if the objective is maximizing ROI. However, this does not necessarily mean that such an MMF is discarded.

Imagine a scenario in which an MMF with a relatively uninteresting SANPV is a necessary precursor to the construction of an MMF that has a strongly positive SANPV. It may still be worth constructing the first MMF (even if it has a negative SANPV), because it enables us to experience the attractive returns of the second MMF.

Consider the table in Figure 3.5. In this analysis we've identified the interrelations between MMFs in terms of precursors. Precursors come in two types:

- Development precursors: These occur where the facilities of another MMF must be in place before development can be started. This type of precursor therefore requires strictly sequential development.

- Delivery precursors: These occur when an MMF is not useful to the customer in terms of revenue generation until its precursor is in place; however, development of the two MMFs can be undertaken in parallel. This type of precursor therefore opens the possibility of concurrent development, as long as the order of delivery is not reversed.

In the table, MMF B is a development precursor to MMF E (i.e., we can't begin to construct E until B has been completed), but MMF F is a delivery

MMF #	MMF Name	Precursors * Parallel delivery allowed
A	Car Rental	H
B	Hotel Reservation	H
C	Itinerary Planner	A, B, D, F
D	Flight Reservation	H
E	Tour Group Organizer	B, D, F*
F	Local Activities	
G	Vacation Packages	A, B, D, F*
H	Online Payment	
I	Online Calendar	
J	Vacation Planner	C, F

Figure 3.5
Recognizing MMF Precursors

precursor to MMF E (we can develop F in parallel with E, but we can't deliver it until E is delivered).

These precursor dependencies between MMFs are an important part of determining MMF sequencing, a subject more fully dealt with in Chapter 5. It is sometimes helpful to picture these precursors graphically, as illustrated in the next section.

The MMF Precedence Graph

Once the individual MMFs have been evaluated, an MMF precedence graph is constructed. The graph reflects the relative ordering of MMFs, taking into account both delivery and development constraints. The extent to which development constraints are considered depends to some extent on the software process being implemented. The precedence graph therefore reflects the logical ordering among features. Consider the travel agency example again. Common sense business constraints dictate that there would be no point in developing an MMF to handle multiple destination flights, before developing the MMF to handle simple roundtrip flights. A precedence relation would therefore be established between these two MMFs.

A simple way to construct a precedence graph is through building a table and marking all of the precedence relations that exist for each MMF. The table in Figure 3.5 was constructed to identify precedence relationships between MMFs in the travel agency example. Remember, though, that these relationships are defined by the customer, and reflect business and operational constraints on the use of delivered MMFs.

It is simple to then construct a precedence graph from this table. All MMFs containing no precedence relations are placed as opening nodes on the graph. This includes MMFs H, I, and F. Those MMF numbers are then removed from the MMF lists in the right-hand column of table. This then releases a further set of MMFs, including MMFs A, B, and D. Each of these MMFs is added as a node on the graph, and a link is drawn from the MMF to each MMF on which it is dependent. For example, a line is drawn from MMF C to MMFs A, B, D, and F. This process continues until all MMFs have been added to the graph.

Within the MMF precedence graph, the MMFs are represented as nodes, and development constraints as the arcs. The precedence graph established by stakeholders for the online travel agency is depicted in Figure 3.6. The shaded nodes represent MMFs that have no precedence dependencies.

Throughout the book, we use the term "strands" to describe a series of dependent MMFs. For example, in Figure 3.6 the MMFs **H**, **A**, and **G**, form a strand depicted as **HAG**, as do MMFs **F**, **C**, and **J**, depicted as **FCJ**. A smaller section of a strand such as **H**, **HA**, or **AG** is defined as a substrand.

Finally, the precedence relations should be annotated to specify whether the precursor MMF is a development precursor or a delivery precursor (see previous section).

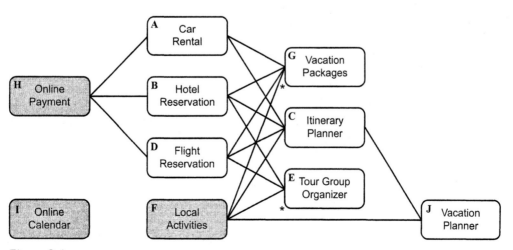

Figure 3.6
An MMF Precedence Graph for the Online Travel Agency

Architectural Precursors

Precursors for MMF development don't necessarily have to be other MMFs. For example, it's not hard to postulate an MMF whose construction requires a particular architectural framework, a specific connectivity solution, or the presence of some third-party off-the-shelf software. Given the rules for identifying MMFs that have been set out earlier in this chapter, precursors of this type would not meet the criteria to be considered an MMF.

Typically these precursors are related to the overall architecture of the solution. They represent a new type of IFM element, distinctly different. These new IFM elements, together with the IFM approach to architecture, are examined in detail in the next chapter.

Summary

- An MMF represents a minimum marketable feature, which is a chunk of functionality that returns specific value to the user.
- MMFs can be identified either through top-down decomposition or by using a bottom-up approach in which an MMF is composed from a number of more primitive features.
- MMFs are represented and analyzed in terms of a set of costs and returns for each period of the project lifecycle.
- A risk analysis covering both development and revenue risks is an essential input to this vector of values.
- NPV calculations are applied to MMF costs and returns to create sequence-adjusted net present values (SANPVs) at each possible development period.
- Many MMFs have precursors that must be identified and characterized according to whether they represent delivery or development dependencies. These can be effectively represented using precedence graphs.

References

1. Manifesto for Agile Software Development, Agile Alliance, http:// agilemanifesto.org

2. Alistair Cockburn, *Agile Software Development*, Reading, Massachusetts: Addison Wesley, 2001.

3. M. Beedle, M. Devos, Y. Sharon, K. Schwaber, J. Sutherland, "SCRUM: An extension pattern language for hyperproductive software development." Chapter taken from *Pattern Languages of Program Design 4*, N. Harrison, B. Foote, and H. Rohnert (eds.), Reading, Massachusetts: Addison Wesley, 1999.

4. K. Schwaber, M. Beedle, and R. Martin, *Agile Software Development with SCRUM*, Upper Saddle River, New Jersey: Prentice Hall, 2001.

5. P. Kruchten, *The Rational Unified Process: An Introduction* (2nd ed.), Reading, Massachusetts: Addison Wesley, 2000.

6. S. Palmer and J. Felsing, *Practical Guide to Feature-Driven Development*, Upper Saddle River, New Jersey: Prentice Hall, 2002.

7. C. K. Chang, S. Hua, J. Cleland-Huang, and A. Kuntzmann-Combelles, "Function-Class Decomposition," *IEEE Computer*, 34(12): December 2001, pp. 87–93.

8. A function class decomposition online tutorial is available at http://icse.cs. iastate.edu

9. P. Klein, "Rationalize This! ROI Strategies Abound," *Information Week*, August 6, 2001.

10. E. Hall, *Managing Risk: Methods for Software Systems Development*, Reading, Massachusetts: Addison Wesley, 1998.

11. B. Boehm, *Software Engineering Economics: Advances in Computing Science and Technology*, Upper Saddle River, New Jersey: Prentice Hall, 1981.

12. R. Pressman, *Software Engineering: A Practitioners Approach*, (5th ed.), New York: McGraw-Hill, 2001.

13. Project Management Institute, *A Guide to the Project Management Body of Knowledge*, 2000.

Incremental Architecture

The place of architecture in the software design process is one of the most hotly debated subjects in computer science today. Some argue that architecture should be defined and validated before development starts, while others argue that it should evolve as the code is written. In this chapter we discuss the concept of incrementally delivered architecture as a tool for optimizing the returns of a software development project, treating architecture as a critical part of the value creation process. IFM principles are then applied to compare the financial benefits of up-front versus evolutionary architecture.■

The Place of Architecture

Few if any subjects in the field of software methodology have stirred up as much debate and ignited as much passion as software architecture. Even the meaning of the term is disputed. Yet most practitioners acknowledge its reality and its importance. The questions relate to how to it is to be defined, where it is to be used, and what authority architectural concerns have in a software development project.

Bass, Clements, and Kazman in their seminal work, *Software Architecture in Practice*, define it as "the structure of structures of the system, which comprise software components, the externally visible properties of those components and the relationships among them." They go on to say that "the intent of this definition is that a software architecture must abstract some information from the system . . . and yet provide enough information to be a basis for analysis, decision making and hence risk reduction"[1].

The traditional RUP position is that the definition of software architecture is a critical part of any development undertaking. High-level architectural options are identified in the inception phase; then the most promising architectural solution is selected and fully defined during the elaboration phase. The Object Management Group's UML version 3.0 definition and specification states that "Architecture provides the organizational structure of a system. As such it can be recursively decomposed into parts with well-defined interfaces and relationships, and constraints that describe how the parts must be assembled. These parts include classes, components and subsystems"[2].

In contrast, the XP/agile software development approach adopts a different position with respect to the place of architecture in the lifecycle. XP dismisses the need for up-front architectural planning and instead moves to code cutting and pairwise programming at the earliest opportunity, arguing that time spent on architectural considerations early in the development lifecycle is not time well spent[3].

The proponents of the agile software development approach believe that early architectural considerations can be both a diversion and a waste of money. Early architecture is perceived as a box into which a solution is unfairly locked before the real parameters are known or understood[4]. In the agile approach, architecture is therefore seen to evolve throughout the development of the system without the benefit of any type of up-front architectural plan. The guiding philosophy is the delivery of the simplest solution needed to implement the current functionality.

Unsurprisingly, the debate has become essentially a religious one, with fervent and passionate adherents to each viewpoint making their respective cases through examples, inference, apocryphal tales, and a variety of principled positions, accompanied by dire warnings.

Architecture versus Rules

One of the most commonly stated positions is the assertion that software architecture is ultimately about standards. Often espoused by developers, this view takes the position that software architecture is an understanding or an approach to be followed by the system, and is often codified by rules. From such a position it is only a short step to suggest that interface and interoperability standards such as Java 2 Enterprise Edition (J2EE) or Microsoft's .Net are by definition software architectures.

We'll revisit this perception of architecture as a set of "big rules" later in the chapter, but for now it's interesting to note that both of the definitions cited in the previous section define software architecture in terms of an assembly of smaller pieces. Bass, Clements, and Kazman call these pieces "components." The Unified Modelling Language (UML) calls them "parts."

This view of architecture as something other than rules, and capable of first-level decomposition, is not new. As early as 1992 Perry and Wolf wrote that software architecture is "a set of architectural (or if you will, design) elements that have a particular form"[5]. Booch, Rumbaugh, and Jackson echo this perception: "An architecture is the set of significant decisions about the organization of a software system, the selection of the structural elements, and their interfaces by which the system is composed, together with their behavior as specified in the collaborations among those elements"[6].

In this section, we adopt this perception of architecture as a set of "elements" and we later refer to architectural elements specifically. However, for the purposes of IFM, we maintain a strictly neutral position on the question of where and how software architecture activities should be performed in the lifecycle.

The Problem with Architecture

In his book *The Timeless Way of Building*, from his seminal trilogy on constructional architecture, Christopher Alexander asserts that no architecture is ever perfect, despite our best efforts. He demonstrates that first-stage architectural predictions are generally wrong, recognizing that "people tend to end up using buildings differently from the way they thought they would." He goes on to point out that as the pieces become larger, this creates a more serious problem[7].

We must recognize at the outset, therefore, that software architecture, however it is motivated, is at best predictive guesswork. While this may fly in the face of adherents to the traditions of RUP, it is the pragmatic reality. Successful software architects have generally become successful not through their ability to follow process, but through their intuitive assessment of business problems and their experience and understanding of how those can be solved through information technology. Often their success comes from their very creativity, rather than their methodological adherence.

In any serious software development project, the architecture of the system is best thought of as a living entity that must be adapted in response to ever-changing system requirements, to feedback from prototyping efforts and systems tests, and as a result of deeper understanding gained for the nonfunctional requirements of the system.

This is not to suggest that early architectural definition is unnecessary. In the world of building construction we have by no means rejected the role of the architect despite Christopher Alexander's assertion that ultimately building usage is often out of compliance with architectural objectives. Indeed we would not contemplate attempting any serious construction without first considering and satisfying the architectural prerequisites.

The difference between constructing buildings and writing software is that it is much easier and less costly to adjust the architecture during construction of a software system than it is during the construction of a physical building. This suggests that software architecture exhibits the unusual quality of being simultaneously a prerequisite to development, while at the same time subject to ongoing and iterative correction. As Busse and Hecksel have observed, the creation of architecture-centric iterative development processes would appear to be greatly beneficial[8].

We have attempted to capture this tension in IFM by describing architecture as something that can be defined early, while resisting the mandatory instantiation of all architectural elements for exactly the reasons outlined by Busse and Hecksel. As we stated earlier, IFM takes a neutral approach to when architecture is actually defined. Chapter 8 describes the RUP approach, in which architecture is defined early, while Chapter 9 describes the agile approach, in which architecture is evolved throughout the development phase. As we will see in the following sections, the critical issue to IFM is not so much when the architecture is defined, as when it is developed and delivered.

Pieces of the Pattern

Clearly, the definition of architecture as a piecewise or iterative process raises significant cause-and-effect questions about its usefulness to the software development effort. While the proponents of XP may be comfortable with positioning architecture as the outcome of programming efforts and may take comfort in the fluidity of an iterative and gradually emerging architecture, we are left with the sense that if architecture is merely a byproduct of design and construction, its usefulness as a guide to that design and construction must be somewhat limited. It you don't need architecture to be successful in writing software, why have it at all?

There are several possible responses to this question, but one of the most interesting can be found in the principles of Sun Microsystems' SunTone AM[9]. SunTone AM adheres to the three main tenets of RUP: use case, architecture, and iterative development. Unlike RUP, it argues that architecture is primarily necessary to create a framework for patterns-based development and for the delivery of predictable, nonfunctional characteristics or system qualities. This, according to SunTone AM, is the key to achieving low-risk, predictable time to market.

While SunTone AM certainly presents a compelling case for the benefits of patterns-based development, it does not address the cost and benefits analysis of up-front architectural efforts. We need a way to measure the cost effectiveness of defining patterns early in the lifecycle at a stage when so little is known about the performance and behavior of the yet-to-be-constructed system. What is missing here is the ability to trace benefits back to business priorities, a financial driver, if you will, that would allow architectural benefit to be visible and measurable to the project's stakeholders.

Boehm et al. recognized this and identified three necessary factors from which a software system can be developed[10]. These can be summarized as follows:

- The software and system components, interconnections, and constraints that collectively will compose the physical system
- The user requirements of the system stakeholders expressed in the form of needs statements
- The rationale demonstrating that the proposed components, interconnections, and constraints would satisfy the expressed needs of the system stakeholders

A Value-Driven Approach

IFM recognizes that architecture needs unambiguous traceability back to the needs of the stakeholders so that the rationale behind each architectural element is well-defined. In line with its core principles, IFM ascribes value to software architecture in terms of its impact on ROI, rather than in terms of development purity or refactoring ease. This value-driven approach requires some kind of ROI analysis for architecture.

Clearly, it is not possible to define an ROI for architecture without significant decomposition of the problem and a redefinition of the place of architecture within the ROI measurement. The following sections describe how this can be achieved.

The Codependency of Architecture

Software developers and development managers like to believe that architectures establish "big rules" to be followed by programming staff during the construction phase of the project. The idea is that the definition of top-level interfaces and major software components will provide the necessary constraints in which developers can perform their work. These constraints are designed to ensure that systemwide components will communicate effectively with each other and, hopefully, that they will form a coherent whole.

For example, an architectural decision might be taken to use Java Servlet Pages (JSPs), rather than Active Server Pages (ASPs) in the Web server tier of a multitier Web-facing application. Such a decision determines the type of Web-server technology to be used and the programming environment for the logic in this tier of the application. It also constrains to some extent the type of Web server to be used and the hardware platform on which it can be deployed.

Similarly, an architect may determine that the business logic tier will involve synchronous rather than asynchronous messaging. Or an architect may decide that a J2EE and Enterprise Java Beans (EJB) environment will be used but with certain constraints applied—for example, Session Beans will be used but not Entity Beans. Each such decision impacts the nonfunctional requirements of the system (its ability to scale, to be predictable, to be manageable, etc.) before any lines of code have been written. To some extent each such decision also constrains the type of code to be written and the programming language to be used. We're unlikely to be writing in Visual Basic if the business logic tier consists mostly of EJBs, for example.

In reality, things are not quite this simple. The software architecture provides a broad-brush definition of the overall solution and its initial top-down decomposition; however, it may not provide sufficient detail to forecast the behavior of the solution's systemic qualities, such as performance and latency. The architect has to either build extensive performance models or rely on crafted code from the developer in order to validate the architecture, make accurate predictions, and, if necessary, institute mid-course corrections. This process is depicted in Figure 4.1.

Architecture-centric methodologies partially address this concern by pulling selected parts of the construction phase into the elaboration phase, under the guise of a "proof of concept." The idea turns out to be relatively sound in practice. The architect picks the use cases that are thought to be the most

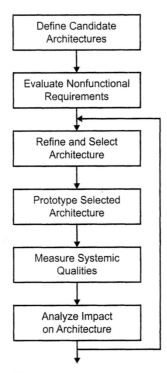

Figure 4.1
The Co-dependency of Architecture

troublesome from a system qualities perspective and implements them in prototype form end-to-end. By building in appropriate metrics, the architect can infer overall system performance, construct a model of nonfunctional characteristics (usually a statistical model), and test key interfaces.

As an approach it has much in its favor, but its greatest weakness is that the selection of those critical use cases is entirely at the discretion of the architect. The architect must be experienced enough to be able to recognize and select the most troublesome use cases—there is no heuristic or methodology to assist in that selection. It is at best an intuitive approach that leaves the architect as much dependent on the code from the developer as the developer is supposedly dependent on the output of the architect.

Taking Architecture in Easy Stages

It's curious that despite the rapid evolution of the concepts of iterative software development, the idea of software architecture as a self-defining monolithic whole has remained unchallenged in the minds of many practitioners for so long. There is, after all, nothing magical about architecture. At first sight, it's just another perspective of the overall solution, and as such it can be subject to iterative definition in the same way that a use-case perspective, or a nonfunctional-requirements perspective emerges over time.

Architecture differs in the strength of its dependencies. One simple architectural definition can affect thousands of lines of code, or even dictate the programming language in which that code is written. It sets up the framework for making decisions about the code and patterns that will be used to develop the system. Changing these decisions mid-stream can be painful, costly, and frustrating.

From a technical perspective it is hard to countenance an iteratively defined architecture. There does not seem to be an appropriate rationale to guide a technical decomposition of the problem into architectural pieces (beyond perhaps the basic layers and tiers of the cube model used by SunTone AM). For this reason, the idea of iteratively defining the architecture, which itself defines the framework for iterations, may be hard to accept. It has all the characteristics of a chicken and egg problem!

A Different Decomposition

IFM, however, does not attempt to decompose an application in this way. Instead the unit of decomposition is the MMF. All applications are defined in terms of their MMFs.

As discussed in Chapter 3, MMFs come with a variety of dependencies. For example, any specific MMF may be dependent on the implementation of prior MMFs in its sequence. In addition, an MMF has quantifiable and measurable impact on the total net present value of the system. It is only a very small step from here to suggest that MMFs also have architectural dependencies. These are links, if you will, to pieces of the overall architecture that are essential for the implementation of the MMF.

Within IFM, these pieces of the architecture are called architectural elements (AEs). In every respect they are treated identically to MMFs and they are sequenced by the same financially driven processes. Their only distinguishing feature is that unlike MMFs they do not themselves return any revenue. They are purely cost elements in the model.

Within such a scenario, small and tightly scoped architectural decisions can be made regarding each MMF. The cost of the architectural prerequisites can be measured and factored into the development cost of the MMF, and

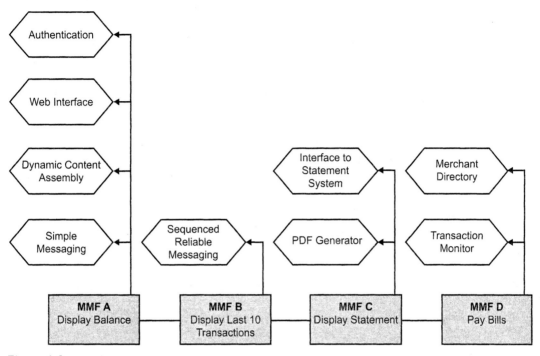

Figure 4.2
Architectural Dependencies in an Example Four-MMF Strand

this information then feeds back into the MMF sequencing decision tree. In effect, MMFs "pull" their architectural dependencies with them as they are sequenced. This is clearly depicted in the example of four MMFs shown in Figure 4.2. In this case, each MMF depends on one or more AEs to provide services such as simple messaging, Web interfaces, or authentication.

This approach to architecture has a number of benefits.

First, it acknowledges the importance of software architecture. IFM sequences both AEs and MMFs.

Second, IFM provides a framework in which architecture is considered within the overall financial analysis. This means that the architectural definition of the system must be broken out into its essential elements in the manner set out in the first section. Architecture can still be envisioned as a set of big rules and described in terms of architectural styles, but those rules and styles are instantiated throughout each individual architectural component.

Third, IFM puts a price on architecture. By factoring architectural costs into the sequencing cost base, we ensure that architecture is subject to the same cost-benefit analysis that occurs for all other aspects of software development.

Fourth, IFM introduces the concept of iterative architectural instantiation. Rather than bringing into being all aspects of the system's architecture at once, IFM uses sequencing strategies to identify the optimal time for instantiating each piece of the architecture. The objective is to develop architectural components as they are needed to support the functionality of each MMF, while optimizing the financial returns of the project. In this respect IFM adopts an agile, or responsive, approach to software architecture.

Fifth, IFM establishes a capacity for options within the architecture. We only create, or spend time creating, those parts of the software architecture that appear within the selected sequencing. AEs that do not appear in the sequence and that are therefore not needed, are simply not constructed. In this respect, it acknowledges the validity of the XP position that architecture should not be created until it's actually needed to support code in production.

The table in Figure 4.3 shows an IFM analysis of a project performed over 16 periods. To help distinguish the different IFM elements, we've identified MMFs by letters and AEs by numbers. In this example, all the AEs take just one period to develop, while the MMFs require anywhere from one to three periods. This is depicted in the table as periods of negative returns.

Figure 4.4 shows what the precursors table for this set of IFM elements might look like. In this example, MMF A requires AE 1, MMFs D and E require AE 2, and MMF F requires AE 3.

Element	Period															
	1	2	3	4	5	6	7	8	9	10	11	12	13	14	15	16
1	-200	0	0	0	0	0	0	0	0	0	0	0	0	0	0	0
A	-200	100	100	90	80	70	60	50	40	30	20	10	0	0	0	0
B	-200	-200	100	130	160	190	220	250	250	250	250	250	250	250	250	250
C	-200	-200	-100	140	180	220	260	300	340	380	400	400	400	400	400	400
2	-400	0	0	0	0	0	0	0	0	0	0	0	0	0	0	0
D	-250	-250	50	80	100	120	140	160	180	200	200	200	200	200	200	200
E	-350	-350	50	100	150	200	250	300	350	350	350	350	350	350	350	350
3	-200	0	0	0	0	0	0	0	0	0	0	0	0	0	0	0
F	-100	-100	100	100	150	150	150	150	150	150	150	150	150	150	150	150

Figure 4.3
An Example Set of MMFs (A–F) and AEs (1–3) (in $US Thousands)

MMF/AE	Precursor
1	
A	1
B	A
C	B
2	
D	2
E	2
3	
F	3

Figure 4.4
Precursors Table Showing Dependencies on AEs and other MMFs

One-to-Many Dependencies in Architecture

In the previous section we observed that MMFs may have architectural precursors—a set of architectural prerequisites that need to be satisfied in order to bring the MMF into being. In conformity with the basic tenets of IFM, we treat these architectural elements like MMFs and factor them into the sequencing decision tree, rather than dumping all architectural prerequisites into a bucket labeled "up-front costs."

But what if more than one MMF requires the same architectural prerequisites? For example, one MMF appearing substantially as business logic in a multi-tier system may depend on the existence of an asynchronous messaging interface in order to communicate with backend mainframes. Suppose another MMF also requires asynchronous messaging, either for the same purpose or for a different purpose, such as communicating with a transaction logger.

As far as the dependency tree is concerned, there is no problem with this. The sequencing process has to satisfy all the prerequisites by placing precursor architectural elements in the sequence ahead of their dependent MMFs. This situation is clearly depicted in Figure 4.4, in which MMFs D and E both have AE 2 as a precursor.

In other words, the impact of bringing the messaging system into play as an architectural element is factored into the sequencing process in terms of costs and time. Once a particular AE has been instantiated it becomes available to all MMFs that may need it, just as would be the case for an MMF precursor.

There is therefore no impact in the sequencing process of an architectural one-to-many dependency. By treating AEs as IFM elements to be sequenced, the NPV is optimized while simultaneously ensuring that all AE precursors are satisfied prior to the construction of their dependent MMFs. In a later section we discuss the possibilities for concurrent sequencing and delivery of these IFM elements.

Architectural Coherency

This incremental, as-needed approach to satisfying architectural considerations may contribute towards optimizing the NPV of the project, but it is insufficient to ensure the coherency of the overall solution. While IFM espouses agility in architecture, that agility exists for reasons of financial efficiency—it is not intended to be a rationale for failing to adopt a coherent architectural approach.

If architecture is considered only in terms of sequenceable AEs, there is a risk that architectural dependencies may conflict or become contradictory.

Imagine a scenario in which there are two MMFs associated with the delivery of synthesized dynamic content to an HTML (Web) client (i.e., automated content delivery from multiple information sources). The option exists to assemble the content within the Web server tier of the system and deliver it as a single HTML stream, or instead to construct a frames-based environment on the client and stream the content independently to the two frames. Figure 4.5 illustrates these two options.

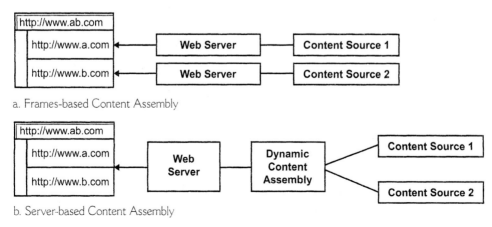

a. Frames-based Content Assembly

b. Server-based Content Assembly

Figure 4.5
Content Assembly Options

Either approach is possible and each has its advantages and disadvantages. It may, however, be less coherent to list a frames-based HTML delivery environment (we'll call this AE 1) as an architectural prerequisite for MMF A, and a server-based content assembly engine (we'll call this AE 2) as an architectural prerequisite for MMF B. If the cost of the server-based content assembly engine were high, that incoherency would reveal itself as a substantially less favorable SANPV for the substrand **2B** versus **1A** (assuming the returns are comparable) and would skew the sequencing decision tree as a result.

Now there may be circumstances in which we actually do want to take such an approach. For example, as a matter of strategy, the more expeditious frames-based approach might be thought acceptable for MMF A because of its benefits in terms of reduced time to market. The introduction of the more complicated server-based content assembly could be delayed until needed later in the project.

IFM provides an excellent way to quantify this decision by comparing the SANPVs of the substrands **1A2B** with **2AB**. It also enables rigorous decision-tree analysis in which the financial benefits of introducing other functionality related to MMFs C, D, and E can be compared against MMF B for cost effectiveness.

However, the architect may feel that there are overriding factors associated with support or scalability, which dictate that the same basic approach to content assembly should be taken through the project. Such a decision requires the review and, if necessary, the modification of architectural dependencies by the project's chief architect.

Nevertheless, IFM provides the opportunity to factor well-informed financial inputs into the decision-making process, rather than proceeding solely on the basis of principled views. Once the basic financial data associated with the different MMFs is in place, various architectural options may be plugged into the model, and their respective impacts on the project's NPV can be examined. In this way the architect is empowered to make informed decisions and is able to justify architectural coherency decisions in financial as well as technical terms.

Multiple Inheritance in Architecture

To complicate the issue, there are circumstances under which it is unclear which architectural prerequisite is the best option for an individual MMF.

Consider the case in which we have an MMF that depends on the existence of a messaging system. The messaging system can be either asynchronous or synchronous. In this example, other MMFs may require one specific type of message system, but this particular MMF can be constructed using either one.

Similarly, a financial portal may offer both bill payment and funds transfer facilities. The bill payment facility may uniquely require a merchant directory, and the funds transfer facilities may uniquely require an interface to some money transfer service such as SWIFT, but both will require access to a transaction monitor for integrity guarantees. This situation is illustrated in Figure 4.6.

Returning again to the tenets of IFM, we want to resolve this conflict through ROI considerations. As it is unlikely that the two types of message system have identical costs, we are faced with the prospect of handling multiple independent cost bases for a single MMF. This is clearly not desirable because we need an unambiguously specified NPV for each IFM element in order to identify an optimal delivery sequence.

However, we do know that selecting the optimal solution to this conflict can best be done when we are actually ready to sequence the MMF in question. We, therefore, invoke the First Architectural Principle of IFM, which can be stated as

"Defer the resolution of any architectural conflict until the time at which the decision is necessary."

Actually this is just a restatement of Capablanca's next move principle:

"There is only one move that really counts: The next one"[15].

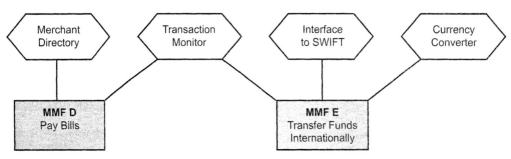

Figure 4.6
MMFs with Multiple Inheritance

To adopt this principle, we wait until all the MMF's predecessors have been scheduled and this MMF becomes available as a candidate for selection. At that point, we evaluate the current architectural portfolio to see if we already have one or the other type of messaging system in place. If we do, we simply use whatever we have in place. If we don't, we duplicate the MMF and assign one of the architectural options to each of the resulting duplicates. We then compare the NPV of project-wide delivery sequences using each of the two potential architectures.

Spiral Architecture

The concept of incrementally defining the key attributes of a software system is not new. Barry Boehm, in "Spiral Model of Development and Enhancement"[11] sets out an incremental delivery model for software development. The spiral model and its associated COCOMO methodology[12] provide invaluable mechanisms for evaluating the choices in incremental delivery.

However, it is characteristic of the spiral model that the key decision drivers are associated with risk. "The spiral model['s] . . . main distinguishing feature . . . is that it creates a risk-driven approach for guiding the software process, rather than a strictly specification-driven or prototype-driven process"[11].

What IFM does is adopt and adapt the iterative approach so that ROI and risk factors work synergistically to drive the process. These ideas are discussed more thoroughly in the following chapters.

Tom Gilb, in *Principles of Software Engineering Management*[13], addresses the benefits and pitfalls of evolutionary delivery. He establishes that evolutionary delivery is neither new nor unexpected in the field of software engineering. Without addressing software architecture specifically, he shows that all aspects of software delivery are required to adopt an evolutionary paradigm and demonstrates it by reference to several studies:

> "Building a system using a well-modularized top-down approach requires that the problem and its solution be well understood. Even if the implementers have previously undertaken a similar project, it is still difficult to achieve a good design for a new system on the first try. Furthermore, the design flaws do not show up until the implementation is well under way so that correcting problems can require major effort"[14].

Summary

- IFM recognizes the importance of software architecture.

- IFM decomposes architecture into a set of architectural elements (AEs) specified in the same way as MMFs.

- IFM ascribes costs and time to AEs and feeds them as costs into the sequencing model.

- IFM creates software architecture incrementally according to the ROI-driven process of sequencing.

- IFM resolves architectural conflicts through cost and NPV comparison and through the application of the first architectural principle.

References

1. Len Bass, Paul Clements, and Rick Kazman, *Software Architecture in Practice,* Reading, Massachusetts: Addison Wesley, 1997.

2. OMG (Object Management Group), UML Definition & Specification version 1.3. Available online at: http://www.omg.org/uml

3. Kent Beck, *Extreme Programming Explained,* Reading, Massachusetts: Addison Wesley, 1999.

4. Scott W. Ambler, "Agile Architectural Modeling," essay from "The Official Agile Modeling (AM) Site," copyright 2001–2002, available online at: http://www. agilemodeling.com/essays/agileArchitecture.htm

5. Dewayne E. Perry and Alexander L. Wolf, "Foundations for the Study of Software Architecture," *ACM SIGSOFT Software Engineering News* 17(4): October 1992.

6. Grady Booch, James Rumbaugh, and Ivor Jacobson, *The UML Modeling Language User Guide,* Reading, Massachusetts: Addison Wesley, 1999.

7. Additional comments on Christopher Alexander's *The Timeless Way of Building* are available online at http://www.interbiznet.com/ern/archives/020724.html

8. Kenn Busse and David Hecksel, "Applying an Architecture Centric Iterative Development Process to the Java Platform," Java One proceedings, 2001. Available online at: http://servlet.java.sun.com/javaone/conf/sessions/2186/google-sf2001.jsp

9. The SunTone Architecture Methodology is available online at: http://www.sun.com/service/sunps/jdc/suntonearchmethod.html

10. Barry W. Boehm, et al., USC Center for Software Engineering, "How Do You Define Software Architecture," 1995. Available online at: http://www.sei.cmu.edu/architecture/definitions.html

11. Barry W. Boehm, "A Spiral Model of Development and Enhancement," *ACM SIGSOFT* 11(5): 61–72, August 1986.

12. Barry W. Boehm, *Software Engineering Economics*, Upper Saddle River, New Jersey: Prentice Hall, 1981.

13. Tom Gilb, *Principles of Software Engineering Management*, Reading, Masssachusetts: Addison Wesley, 1988.

14. Victor Basili and Albert J. Turned, "Iterative Enhancement: A Practical Technique for Software Development," Transactions on Software Engineering (SE-1), No. 4, 1975.

15. Widely attributed to Jose Raul Capablanca Y Granperra (1988–1942) ,World Chess Champion 1921–1927. Quoted from principle 6 of evolutionary delivery in "Evolutionary Project Management–Advanced Theory and Practical Experiences," by Tom Gilb, 1999. Available online at: http://www.spipartners.nl/data/Evo99.PDF

IFM Sequencing Strategies

IFM supports an ROI-informed approach to software development. Project-level ROI is optimized through the delivery of carefully prioritized and customer-valued features, in a sequence driven by the IFM heuristic. Changes in the development plan can be evaluated and justified against the optimal delivery strategy.■

Delivering Valued Features

At the heart of IFM lies the ability to deliver functionality to the customer in a way that maximizes the value of the delivered product. This chapter describes the mechanics of identifying an MMF delivery sequence in order to accomplish this goal. For any given set of MMFs there are numerous feasible sequences, and using a brute-force approach to computing the ROI for each sequence would be extremely time-consuming for projects with more than a trivial number of MMFs. The problem is complicated by the fact that costs and revenues cannot simply be calculated for each MMF as if it were an independent component. These values are dependent on the individual characteristics of the MMF, the positioning within the delivery sequence, and the actual time at which the MMF is completed and delivered to the customer.

As it turns out, the IFM sequencing problem belongs to a category of computer science problems for which there are no known algorithmic solutions. It's necessary to compute and compare all possible combinations. This type of exhaustive computation typically requires an unreasonably long time to run on a computer[1,2].

Therefore, without actually calculating the ROI for every conceivable delivery sequence, we cannot always guarantee that the optimum sequence has been identified. However, by applying the heuristic described in this chapter, we can identify a solid delivery scheme that approaches optimal delivery and for which ROI projections, intangible benefits, and related risks have been carefully analyzed. A more formal empirical analysis of the performance of the IFM heuristic is available at the IFM Web site[8]. The remainder of this chapter describes how the IFM sequencing heuristic works and discusses special circumstances that might require the promotion or demotion of certain MMFs in the delivery sequence.

Cost versus Value Analysis

Developing an MMF is both a cost-incurring and a revenue-generating activity. Usually functionality that delivers higher value versus cost is favored over functionality that returns less value versus cost[3,4]. Unfortunately, existing software development models do not provide a cost-benefit analysis rigorous enough to consistently identify the optimal delivery sequence.

Consider the graph in Figure 5.1, in which each MMF is plotted according to its relative cost and revenue. The most interesting MMFs are those that exhibit the highest value to cost ratio[5]. These are found in the upper-left-hand section of the graph. Selecting an MMF from this area is appealing because it promises significant returns for a relatively small cost. However, the graph does not support the detailed analysis needed to identify an optimal delivery sequence. It suggests MMFs that might be more profitable to develop, but it falls short of the level of analysis required to clearly explain the benefits of alternate project schedules.

In reality, MMF sequencing must carefully balance numerous factors related not just to a single MMF but also to a complete sequence of them. An added complication arises because certain MMFs are time sensitive, meaning that their ROI can be significantly impacted by the delivery schedule. In these cases it sometimes pays to deliver a lower-valued MMF earlier in the schedule so as to capture its optimal revenue potential. Another weakness of this approach is that the graph does not capture the intangible benefits of each MMF or its architectural precursors.

Interestingly, IFM analysis will demonstrate that there is sometimes a trade-off between optimizing cash flow and maximizing ROI. IFM takes the

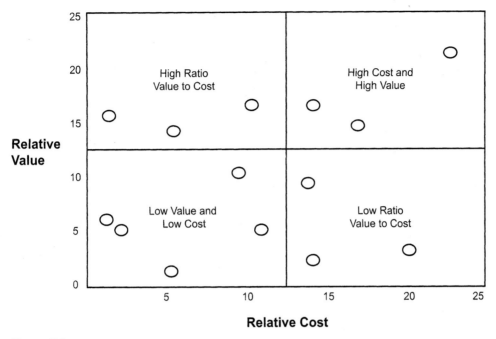

Figure 5.1
Value versus Cost for an MMF

approach that the primary goal is maximizing project NPV, but it also provides sufficient information to enable informed decisions about cash flow.
Proponents of agile software development who follow the maxim of always
selecting the simplest possible design, tend to optimize for cash flow—
unfortunately without the benefits of IFM analysis to determine how this
will impact other project level factors such as NPV[6,7].

Cost-Benefit Analysis of an MMF Delivery Sequence

As we already discussed, MMFs come in many different shapes and sizes. To
introduce the concepts related to the cost-benefit analysis of an MMF we first
consider a standard case in which five MMFs, labeled A through E, follow a
similar pattern of projected revenue generation. Each one of them incurs an
initial development cost, followed by a period of income generation in
which income increases gradually over time.

The five MMFs also have precedence relationships. MMF A must be delivered prior to MMF B, and MMF B prior to MMF C. Similarly, MMF D must
be delivered prior to MMF E. Figure 5.2 illustrates this scenario. Within this

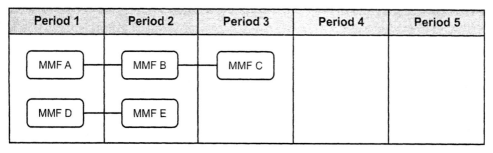

a. An MMF Precedence Graph

MMF	PERIOD							
	1	2	3	4	5	6	7	8
A	-100	80	81	82	83	84	85	86
B	-50	100	102	104	106	108	110	112
C	-200	75	76	77	78	79	80	81
D	-75	100	102	104	106	108	110	112
E	-100	60	61	62	63	64	65	66

b. Revenue per Period

Figure 5.2
MMF Precedence Graph and Related Cost & Revenue Projections (in $US Thousands)

scenario there are nine potential delivery sequences available, including **ABCDE, ADBEC,** and **DEABC.**

From the individual costs and revenues shown in Figure 5.2b, we see that MMF B appears to be the most interesting one. With an initial development cost of $50,000, it is projected to return approximately $100,000 per period following its delivery, with gradual increases in revenue. However, the precedence graph shows that MMF A is a precursor to MMF B, meaning that we must deliver the rather uninteresting MMF A in order to reap the rewards of MMF B. On the other branch of the graph, MMF D costs $75,000 to deliver and returns the same revenue as MMF B. This is also interesting, because despite MMF D's slightly higher development costs it has no precedence dependency and can therefore start delivering value one period earlier. It is certainly not intuitively obvious whether it makes more sense to deliver MMFs A and B first, or MMF D.

For now, let's just focus on these three MMFs, delivered sequentially over the first three periods, followed by five periods of additional revenue generation. In this example, we assume that each period is three months long. We also assume a discount rate of 10% per year, which translates to 2.41% per quarter $(1.241^4 \sim = 1.1)$, and we'll use this figure to calculate the NPV of each delivery option. This follows the techniques explained in Figure 2.2 from Chapter 2.

Given these assumptions, Figure 5.3 shows that the delivery sequence **ABD** results in an NPV of $1,304,000, compared with the Figure 5.4 ordering of **DAB** and related NPV value of $1,328,000. In this case, the second delivery sequence of **DAB** appears to pay off, albeit not by a large margin. Interestingly, in this example, the sequence of **ADB** shown in Figure 5.5 produces almost identical results to **ABD**.

Another observation, one which will be considered in more detail later, is that sometimes delivery of an entire path such as **ABC** or **DE** as a single unit can reduce the overall ROI of the project. This usually occurs when one of the MMFs on the right-hand side of the path has a poor value-to-cost ratio and eats up valuable resources without returning significant revenue.

Sequence	MMF	1	2	3	4	5	6	7	8	Net
ABD	A	-100	80	81	82	83	84	85	86	481
	B		-50	100	102	104	106	108	110	580
	D			-75	100	102	104	106	108	445
Cash		-100	30	106	284	289	294	299	304	1,506
PV @	2.41%	-98	29	99	258	257	255	253	251	1,304

Figure 5.3
NPV for Delivery Sequence of **ABD** (Rounded to $US in Thousands)

Sequence	MMF	1	2	3	4	5	6	7	8	Net
DAB	D	-75	100	102	104	106	108	110	112	667
	A		-100	80	81	82	83	84	85	395
	B			-50	100	102	104	106	108	470
Cash		-75	0	132	285	290	295	300	305	1,532
PV @	2.41%	-73	0	123	259	257	256	254	252	1,328

Figure 5.4
NPV for Delivery Sequence of **DAB** (Rounded to $US in Thousands)

Sequence	MMF	1	2	3	4	5	6	7	8	Net
ADB	A	-100	80	81	82	83	84	85	86	481
	D		-75	100	102	104	106	108	110	555
	B			-50	100	102	104	106	108	470
Cash		-100	5	131	284	289	294	299	304	1,506
PV @	2.41%	-98	5	122	258	257	255	253	251	1,303

Figure 5.5
NPV for delivery sequence **ADB** (Rounded to $US in Thousands)

The Complexity of the Task

The main problem in identifying the optimal delivery sequence is that computing and comparing each feasible schedule for complex projects is just too time-consuming. For a project with only three MMFs (A, B, and C) there would be six feasible delivery sequences (**ABC, ACB, BAC, BCA, CAB,** and **CBA**) plus additional shorter sequences, or "strands" (such as **AB** and **AC**). In this case we could quite easily analyze all the possibilities in order to determine the optimal one.

Similarly, for a project with four MMFs and no precursor constraints, there would be 24 possible delivery sequences, again something easily handled by an automated tool. However, the number of feasible delivery sequences increases exponentially as the number of MMFs increases. The number is constrained by the precursor relationships, but the upper bound is the factorial of the number of MMFs. Five MMFs would result in 5! ($5 \times 4 \times 3 \times 2 \times 1 = 120$), and six MMFs would be 720 ($6! = 6 \times 5 \times 4 \times 3 \times 2 \times 1$). A project with 20 MMFs has an upper bound of 2,432,902,008,176,640,000 delivery sequences! It would be infeasible to examine this number of sequences in a reasonable amount of time, even with an exceptionally high-speed computer. These numbers are summarized in Figure 5.6.

Therefore in complex projects with several MMFs, the infeasibility of performing an exhaustive analysis to identify the optimal delivery sequence suggests the need for a heuristic approach. IFM uses a heuristic in which a set of rules is applied to identify a good solid delivery sequence. We'll be taking a look at that heuristic shortly.

No. of MMFs	No. of Feasible Sequences	No. of MMFs	No. of Feasible Sequences
1	1	11	39,916,800
2	2	12	479,001,600
3	6	13	6,227,020,800
4	24	14	87,178,291,200
5	120	15	1,307,674,368,000
6	720	16	20,922,789,888,000
7	5,040	17	355,687,428,096,000
8	40,320	18	6,402,373,705,728,000
9	362,880	19	121,645,100,408,832,000
10	3,628,800	20	2,432,902,008,176,640,000

Figure 5.6
Upper Bound of Feasible Delivery Sequences for a Set of MMFs

MMF Sequencing Strategies

In this section we explore two basic approaches to MMF sequencing. The first strategy is described as a "greedy" approach, in which only MMFs with no unresolved precursors are considered for selection. From this subgroup, the one with the greatest NPV is then selected. The greedy heuristic might intuitively be taken by customers and developers if they select an MMF without the benefit of a full NPV analysis. As we shall see shortly, this approach does not tend to perform very well. It is described below primarily to demonstrate why it may fail to deliver optimal returns.

The second method involves a look-ahead approach in which the composite NPV of a sequence of adjacent MMFs, known as a strand, is considered. Each strand is negatively weighted according to the number of its required development periods, and the strand with the highest-weighted NPV is selected for development. As we shall see, this second algorithm identifies a delivery sequence that returns much closer to optimal ROI and in many cases identifies the optimal sequence itself. We refer to this approach as the IFM heuristic.

Both techniques are discussed in more detail in the following sections. To introduce these two approaches we make a few initial significant simplifications in order to explain the methods succinctly. First, we assume that the development of each MMF takes exactly one period. Second, we assume that one and only one MMF is developed during each period. Finally, we describe each approach in terms of MMFs only, then later evaluate some candidate heuristics to see how well they perform in the presence of architectural elements. More realistic examples, in which MMFs exhibit more challenging behaviors, are introduced in Chapter 6.

The Greedy Approach

The greedy approach is a shortsighted method that selects the next MMF by considering only those MMFs for which no unfulfilled precursors exist. If a precursor MMF has already been scheduled, the precursor is said to have been fulfilled. From the subset of MMFs with no unfulfilled precursors, the one with the highest NPV over the remaining periods is selected.

Consider the MMFs shown in Figure 5.7 and assume they follow the same precedence relationships as those of Figure 5.2 (e.g., ABC and DE). For this example we shall also assume the discount rate of 2.41% per period and

MMF	Costs	Revenue per Period	SANPV if Development Starts in Period						
			1	2	3	4	5	6	7
A	-50	45	231	189	149	109	70	32	-5
B	-40	60	334	278	223	169	117	66	16
C	-20	35	198	165	133	102	71	41	12
D	-50	50	262	216	170	126	83	40	-1
E	-60	30	128	101	74	48	23	-2	-26

Figure 5.7
Sequence Adjusted NPVs Assuming 2.41% / Period (Rounded to $US in Thousands)

make one further assumption that revenue is returned at a constant rate throughout all periods following delivery. For example, MMF A costs $50,000 to develop and returns $45,000 per period following delivery.

We can calculate the SANPV for each MMF representing the NPV of the cash flow that would be generated if development of the MMF were started in the specified period. In this case, because each MMF in the example requires only one development period, delivery occurs at the end of the same period. The method for computing SANPV values is described in Chapter 3. If delivered at the end of period 1, MMF A would return a total of $231,000, whereas if it were delivered at the end of period 2, it would deliver $189,000. Similarly, MMF B would deliver $334,000 if delivered at the end of period 1.

Applying the greedy approach, we first have to identify those MMFs that have no precursors and are therefore candidates for selection. MMFs A and D are available. If delivered at the end of period 1, MMF A would return $231,000, whereas MMF D would return $262,000. Therefore, we select MMF D. This means that MMFs A and E are now available for selection. These would deliver $189,000 and $101,000, respectively, if delivered at the end of period 2, and so we select MMF A. MMFs B and E are now available, and B is selected. This process continues until all development slots have been filled up. Using this approach, the identified delivery sequence would be **DABCE**, and the project would have a total NPV of

$$\$262,000 + \$189,000 + \$223,000 + \$102,000 + \$23,000 = \$799,000$$

If a thorough analysis of all feasible delivery options is performed, the optimal delivery sequence turns out to be **ABDCE** with an NPV of $804,000.

Clearly, the main advantage of this approach is its simplicity; its faults are equally obvious. For example, an MMF exhibiting high cost and low revenues could in effect block visibility of more appealing MMFs in its path.

MMF	Costs	Revenue	SANPV if Development Starts in Period						
			1	2	3	4	5	6	7
A	-50	15	44	31	18	6	-6	-18	-30
B	-25	40	224	187	150	114	79	45	12
C	-40	20	85	67	49	32	15	-1	-17

Figure 5.8
Faulting the Greedy Approach (Rounded to $US in Thousands)

Consider the oversimplified situation of three MMFs (A, B, and C) with the costs and returns depicted in Figure 5.8, and for which MMF A is a precursor to MMF B. In this case, MMF A with a development cost of $50,000 and revenues of $15,000 per period blocks the way to the more interesting MMF B with development costs of $25,000 and returns of $40,000 per period. MMF C costs $40,000 and returns $20,000 per period.

Although a full calculation of the three feasible delivery sequences shows that the sequence **ABC** delivers an NPV of $281,000 compared to $267,000 and $262,000 for sequences **CAB** and **ACB** respectively, the greedy algorithm would make the mistake of selecting **CAB**. In a nutshell, the greedy method does not look ahead to see the potential returns of MMF C, because they are hidden by the dismal returns of MMF A.

This problem is especially severe if a strand is initially blocked by an AE. This in effect represents the worst-case scenario in which an element on the left-hand side of a strand incurs cost but returns no measurable value in terms of revenue. We can compensate for this by considering simple AE-MMF pairs as selectable elements, but this still does not solve the primary problem of the greedy method.

A Simple Look-Ahead Approach

A better approach would involve analyzing entire strands and substrands to identify future MMFs that might be more profitable. A precedence graph is composed of a number of these MMF strands. To reach an MMF we first have to develop all of the precursor MMFs in the strand. Again, returning to the precursor relationships defined in Figure 5.2, the set of strands would be **A, AB, ABC, B, BC, C, D, DE,** and **E**. Of course, only the strands without unresolved precursors could be selected for development in any specific period. This means that for the first period analysis, we could only consider the strands **A, AB, ABC, D,** and **DE**.

Strand	SANPV if Development Starts in Period						
	1	2	3	4	5	6	7
A	231	189	149	109	70	32	-5
AB	509	412	318	226	136	48	-38
ABC	642	514	389	267	148	31	-38
B		278	223	169	117	66	16
BC		411	325	240	158	78	-1
C			133	102	71	41	12
D	262	216	170	126	83	40	-1
DE	363	290	219	149	81	14	-51
E		101	74	48	23	-2	-26

Figure 5.9
SANPV for Each Strand @ 2.41% / Period (Rounded to $US in Thousands)

In this simple look-ahead method, analysis is performed on individual strands of MMFs, with the aim of identifying the strand that delivers the highest returns. To accomplish this, the composite NPV is calculated for each strand by summing the individual NPVs for each MMF within the strand at their individual development periods. Figure 5.9 shows the SANPVs for the MMFs introduced in Figure 5.7.

For example, the SANPV value shown under period 1 for the strand **ABC** is calculated as

$$SANPV_{A:\ Period\ 1} + SANPV_{B:\ Period\ 2} + SANPV_{C:\ Period\ 3}$$

which sums to $231,000 + $278,000 + $133,000 = $642,000.

Similarly, the SANPV value shown under period 2 for the same strand of ABC is calculated as

$$SANPV_{A:\ Period\ 2} + SANPV_{B:\ Period\ 3} + SANPV_{C:\ Period\ 4}$$

which sums to $189,000 + $223,000 + $102,000 = $514,000.

Once SANPVs have been calculated for each strand, the analysis proceeds in the same way as the greedy approach. To select the MMF for period one, the SANPV of each strand is analyzed and the highest strand selected. In this case **ABC**, with an SANPV of $642,000, is selected, and MMF A is assigned to period 1 development.

However, this does not necessarily mean that we will deliver MMFs B and C in periods 2 and 3. This heuristic performs NPV analysis on a period-by-period basis and it may discard the **ABC** strand before completing development of the entire strand. To select the MMF for the next period, the SANPVs of the available strands for period 2 are analyzed. As MMF A has already been selected, the top three strands in the table, which all start with MMF A, are removed from consideration. Of the remaining strands for period 2, the strand **BC**, with an SANPV of $411,000, appears most promising, and so B is selected for the second period.

When period 3 is reached, the SANPV of the strand **DE** exceeds the SANPV of **C**, so the heuristic departs from the **ABC** strand and develops MMF D in that period instead.

The process continues until MMFs have been assigned to all the available development slots. In this case, the simple look-ahead approach selects the sequence **ABDCE**, for a total NPV of

$231,000 + $278,000 + $170,000 + $102,000 + $23,000 = $804,000.

An additional study (not shown here) reveals that this is in fact the optimal delivery sequence.

Despite its apparent success in this example, this approach has an important weakness. It is selecting the seemingly best strand without considering development time as a consumable resource. Consider the set of MMFs that appear in Figure 5.10.

In this example we shall assume that MMF A is a precursor to MMF B, and MMF C is a precursor to MMF D. Armed with this precursor information, we can compute the strands and their associated SANPVs in the usual way, resulting in the values shown in Figure 5.11. In this example we have assumed that the periods are months, which means that the assumed discount rate of 10% per year equates to 0.8% per period ($1.008^{12} \sim= 1.1$).

The simple look-ahead heuristic would select the strand **AB** in the first period and go on to identify the delivery sequence **ACBD**. However, this sequence is not the one with the optimal NPV. As shown in Figure 5.12, this sequence is actually ranked sixth overall and achieves only 96% of the optimal NPV represented by sequence **CABD**.

The approach fails because the combined weights of MMFs A and B overpower the single more interesting weight of MMF C. In effect, the approach

MMF	Costs and Revenues per Period							
	1	2	3	4	5	6	7	8
A	-100	150	150	150	150	150	150	150
B	-200	50	50	50	50	50	50	50
C	-100	100	130	160	144	171	198	225
D	-100	30	30	30	30	0	0	0

Figure 5.10
MMF Set that Fails Simple Look-Ahead ($US in Thousands)

Strand	SANPV if Strand Development Starts in Period							
	1	2	3	4	5	6	7	8
A	910	763	617	473	330	187	46	-94
B	138	90	43	-4	-50	-96	-142	-188
AB	1000	806	614	423	233	45	-142	-94
C	981	764	573	410	272	121	-1	-94
D	18	17	17	17	-11	-39	-66	-94
CD	998	781	590	399	234	55	-95	-94

Figure 5.11
SANPV Table that Fails Simple Look-Ahead @ 0.8% / Period (Rounded to $US in Thousands)

NPV Rank	Sequence	NPV $K	% Optimal	Loss $K
1	CABD	1,804	100%	0
2	CAB	1,787	99%	17
3	CAD	1,761	98%	43
4	CADB	1,758	97%	47
5	CA	1,744	97%	60
6	ACBD	1,734	96%	70
7	ACB	1,717	95%	87
8	ACD	1,691	94%	113
9	ACDB	1,687	94%	117
10	AC	1,674	93%	131
11	CDA	1,616	90%	189
12	CDAB	1,612	89%	192
13	ABCD	1,591	88%	214
14	ABC	1,574	87%	231
15	AB	1,000	55%	804
16	CD	998	55%	806
17	C	981	54%	823
18	A	910	50%	894

Figure 5.12
Comparing Simple Look-Ahead with Optimal NPV ($US in Thousands)

does not take into consideration the number of time periods consumed in order to develop the MMF. Even though the strand **AB** delivers the largest NPV, it also consumes two time-period resources, as opposed to the single time period consumed by the strand **C**.

Failure can also occur when the returns from individual MMFs increase dramatically over time, because the SANPV calculations do not differentiate between the distribution of revenue over the remaining periods. A small difference in NPV between two strands might appear insignificant, but if the revenue of one of those strands rises steeply at the end of the evaluation period, delaying that MMF by even one period has a significant impact on NPV.

The Weighted Look-Ahead Approach

The look-ahead approach can be improved by negatively weighting each strand according to the number of time periods required to develop it. This differentiates between strands that return equal NPVs but that are delivered over a different number of development periods. Accuracy in identifying the optimal delivery sequence increases dramatically if this factor is considered.

It turns out that the most effective weighting factor depends on a number of project characteristics, including the shape of the precedence graph and number of development periods within the scope of the analysis. The following formula is used to negatively weight the NPV of a strand:

$$\text{Weighted SANPV} = \text{Nonweighted SANPV} \times (1 - (\text{WF} \times (p - 1)))$$

where 'WF' represents the selected weighting factor and 'p' represents the number of periods in the currently evaluated strand.

Practice suggests that for a 16-period analysis the weighting factor should be set to 10%–15%, while for an eight-period analysis the factor should be set to 20%–25%. A formal analysis and look-up table of optimal weighting factors for a variety of project characteristics can be found at the IFM Web site[8].

For example, a three-period strand **ABC** with a first-period NPV of $100,000 would be weighted by a 10% factor as follows:

$$\text{Weighted SANPV}_{\text{ABC: Period 1}} = \$100,000 \times (1 - (0.1 \times (3 - 1))) = \$80,000$$

while a two-period strand of MMFs **DE** with the same first period NPV of $100,000 would be weighted as follows:

$$\text{Weighted SANPV}_{\text{DE:Period 1}} = \$100,000K \times (1 - (0.1 \times (2 - 1))) = \$90,000$$

In weighted SANPV (WSANPV) terms, the second and shorter strand of **DE** is the more attractive. Figure 5.13 shows the impact of this on the four-MMF example used earlier. When we apply a weighting factor of 10%, the SANPV table is modified as shown in the figure.

It's interesting to note that if the heuristic is run against this set of numbers, the sequence that emerges is **CABD**, which is in fact the optimal sequence.

Because of its superior ability to select optimal MMF sequences, this weighted look-ahead approach is adopted as the IFM sequencing heuristic. Throughout the remainder of this book, we simply refer to it as the IFM heuristic and assume this approach when we refer to IFM sequencing strategies.

Strand	Weighted SANPV per Period							
	1	2	3	4	5	6	7	8
A	910	763	617	473	330	187	46	-94
B	138	90	43	-4	-50	-96	-142	-188
AB	900	726	552	380	210	41	-127	-84
C	981	764	573	410	272	121	-1	-94
D	18	17	17	17	-11	-39	-66	-94
CD	899	703	531	359	210	49	-85	-84

Figure 5.13
WSANPV Values Derived from Figure 5.11 Using 10% Weighting Factor ($US in Thousands)

Sequencing MMFs and AEs

We noted earlier that the greedy approach performs particularly poorly when AEs on the left side of certain strands block visibility to valued MMFs further down the strand. We now examine one further example to see how the IFM heuristic (weighted look-ahead) approach fares under these conditions. To do so, we will reintroduce AEs into the equation.

Figure 5.14 depicts the costs and revenues of the MMFs and AEs in this example, and Figure 5.15 illustrates their dependencies.

First, we introduce a new notation to represent MMFs with multiple development periods (such as MMF B in Figure 5.14). Previously, we used the notation **1AB** to represent the strand consisting of AE 1, followed by MMF A, followed by B. However, this notation fails to capture the information that MMF B takes two periods to develop instead of just one. So we'll now use a period after the MMF or AE name to depict an additional development period. Therefore, **1AB** represents this same strand but carries the additional information concerning the duration of MMF B. Similarly a strand

AE/MMF	Periods															
	1	2	3	4	5	6	7	8	9	10	11	12	13	14	15	16
1	-50	0	0	0	0	0	0	0	0	0	0	0	0	0	0	0
A	-45	10	10	10	10	10	20	20	20	20	20	20	20	20	20	20
B	-20	-20	60	60	60	60	60	60	60	60	60	60	60	60	60	60
2	-15	0	0	0	0	0	0	0	0	0	0	0	0	0	0	0
C	-25	15	15	15	16	16	16	17	17	17	18	18	18	19	19	19
D	-40	18	18	19	19	20	20	20	21	21	22	22	22	23	23	24

Figure 5.14
Costs and Returns for MMFs and AEs ($US in Thousands)

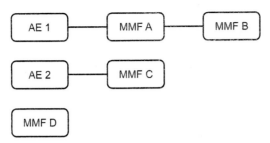

Figure 5.15
Precursor Relationships between AEs and MMFs

such as **E.F..G** would mean that the development of MMF E takes the first two periods, MMF F the next three periods, and MMF G a single period.

Applying the same discount rate of 0.8% and a weighting factor of 10% to calculate the WSANPV array, and assuming analysis over 16 periods, we get the weighted sequence adjusted NPVs for these MMFs shown in Figure 5.16.

The most promising MMF in Figure 5.14 is MMF B; however, this is located at the end of a strand consisting of AE1 and MMF A. Clearly, the greedy approach would not have been able to see this enticing development option. In fact, the only option available to the greedy approach is to select MMF D with NPV $250,000 after which the greedy heuristic terminates! In contrast, the weighted-strand approach enables the IFM heuristic to recognize the value of the strand **1AB.**, despite the costs of AE 1 and the variable revenues of MMF A. The IFM heuristic goes on to select a total delivery sequence of **1AB.D** with a very healthy NPV of $904,000. If all possible, sequences are calculated and compared, this sequence turns out to be within 99% of optimal.

Strand	Period															
	1	2	3	4	5	6	7	8	9	10	11	12	13	14	15	16
1	-50	-49	-49	-48	-48	-48	-47	-47	-47	-46	-46	-45	-45	-45	-44	-44
1A	106	89	73	57	41	25	9	-7	-23	-38	-46	-53	-61	-68	-76	-40
1AB.	519	466	413	361	309	258	207	157	106	57	13	-30	-72	-65	-59	-31
2	-15	-15	-15	-15	-14	-14	-14	-14	-14	-14	-14	-14	-14	-13	-13	-13
2C	161	145	129	114	99	84	70	56	42	29	16	3	-8	-20	-32	-12
D	250	227	205	183	163	142	122	103	84	65	47	30	13	-4	-20	-35

Figure 5.16
WSANPVs for Strands with No Unfulfilled Precursors (Rounded to $US in Thousands)

Risk Mitigation

Because the IFM heuristic sequences MMFs according to their NPV contributions to a project, the fact that risk is factored into the cost-benefit analysis means that high-risk MMFs may appear less attractive and will tend to be deferred within the delivery schedule.

However, IFM takes the approach that once an MMF is selected for development, its individual risks should be mitigated early. The initial risk analysis used to support the MMF's cost-benefit analysis is refined into a full-risk mitigation plan. This identifies the risky parts of the MMF so that they can be tackled early in its development. This also means that an MMF for which anticipated risk mitigation strategies fail may be abandoned.

Iterating the Sequencing Decision

The IFM heuristic is sufficiently adaptable to be used to revisit the sequencing decisions before the start of each MMF/AE iteration. This is useful if revenue projections or other changes to MMF or AE characteristics occur during the project lifecycle.

Changes may occur for a number of reasons. Market conditions may have changed, thereby impacting risk factors either positively or negatively. Business strategies may have been realigned, requiring the reprioritization of MMFs through the promotion of scheduled MMFs to earlier periods within the delivery sequence. Experiences gained through developing the MMFs in the previous period may also impact decisions about future development.

One of the major factors that sometimes causes resequencing is changing risk factors related to the current market environment. As these market risks change, the risk adjustment factors applied to the cost-benefit analysis of impacted MMFs will also change. Certain MMFs may then become more attractive and others less attractive, resulting in the need to reevaluate previous sequencing decisions.

IFM's ability to reevaluate sequencing strategies at each iteration provides financial agility and enables customers to keep their options open. Instead of locking them into a fixed development plan, it supports an incremental approach in which customers can decide step by step which are the best options for their business.

Summary

- The IFM heuristic, which selects the next MMF based on the weighted SANPVs of strands of MMFs, generally performs well. In many cases it returns a sequence close to the optimal NPV for a project, without the need to compute and compare what may be millions of possible delivery sequences.

- The IFM delivery strategies described in this chapter provide the information needed by customers, developers, and managers to make informed decisions and evaluate the impact of these decisions on the project ROI.

- IFM provides an ROI-informed approach to sequencing MMFs.

References

1. Jie Wang, "Average-Case Intractable NP Problems," *Advances in Languages, Algorithms, and Complexity*, Ding-Zhu Du, Ker-I Ko, Dingzhu Du, and Ronald V. Book, eds. New York: Kluwer Academic Publishers, 1997, pp. 313–378.

2. Mark A. Weiss, *Data Structures and Algorithm Analysis in C++* (2nd ed.), Reading, Massachusetts: Addison Wesley, 1999.

3. T. Gilb, *Principles of Software Engineering Management*, Reading, Massachusetts: Addison-Wesley, 1988.

4. H. In and B. Boehm, "Using Win-Win Quality Requirements Management Tools: A Case Study," *Annals of Software Engineering* 11: 141–174, 2001.

5. J. Karlson and K. Ryan, "A Cost-Value Approach for Prioritizing Requirements," *IEEE Software*, 14 (5): 67–74, 1997.

6. Kent Beck, *Extreme Programming Explained: Embrace Change*, Reading, Massachusetts: Addison Wesley, 1999.

7. Don Wells, "Extreme Programming: A Gentle Introduction," January 6, 2003. Available online at: http://www.extremeprogramming.org

8. A look-up table of weighting factors obtained by empirical analysis can be found at the IFM Web site at: http://www.softwarebynumbers.org

MMF Categories and Parallel Development

Costs and revenues of MMFs are influenced by numerous market trends, such as time-to-market constraints, risk mitigation strategies, and anticipated customer usage patterns. These factors must be considered during project planning and MMF sequencing. Concurrent development of MMFs can also improve certain metrics such as overall project delivery time, but may change other critical project characteristics such ROI and initial funding requirements.■

The Impact of MMF Behavior

In Chapter 5 we introduced the IFM heuristic for sequencing MMFs in order to optimize the project NPV and meet other business level objectives. In this chapter we discuss the application of IFM within a realistic market context, in which MMFs do not always behave in a uniform and predictable fashion and in which concurrent development of multiple MMFs may be essential in order to meet deadlines.

Numerous factors can significantly affect the returns of an MMF [1,2], and these can be categorized according to the graphs shown in Figure 6.1. Clearly, many MMFs do not behave in the simplistic fashion described in Chapter 5.

In the first case depicted in Figure 6.1a, the MMF behaves linearly, i.e., revenue is fairly constant following delivery of the MMF. This behavior was exhibited by all the MMFs in the examples in Chapter 5.

In the next two categories, the performance of the MMF is affected by a specific event. Figure 6.1b depicts a case in which an MMF must be delivered

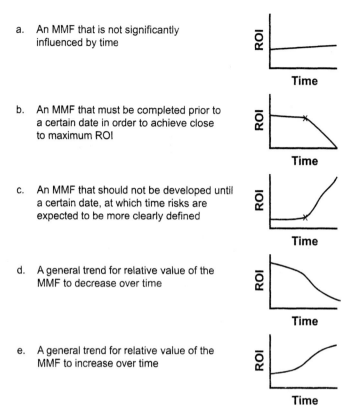

a. An MMF that is not significantly influenced by time

b. An MMF that must be completed prior to a certain date in order to achieve close to maximum ROI

c. An MMF that should not be developed until a certain date, at which time risks are expected to be more clearly defined

d. A general trend for relative value of the MMF to decrease over time

e. A general trend for relative value of the MMF to increase over time

Figure 6.1
Categories of MMF Behavior

prior to a certain event in order for its full potential benefits to be experienced. If this deadline is missed, the anticipated returns will be significantly reduced. For example, we may need to beat a competitor's product to market or complete a software application prior to the grand opening of a new facility. In some cases, such as a head-to-head race with a competitor, delivery projections may need to be continuously updated as new information becomes available.

Figure 6.1c represents the opposite case, in which the development of an MMF should be delayed. This situation might occur when the application being developed requires the use of a new platform or tool that is not yet stable, or when risks cannot be significantly mitigated at the start of the project.

The final two categories represent cases in which revenue either decreases substantially following delivery (Figure 6.1d) or increases substantially (Figure 6.1e). The first case represents a product that might have some sort of gimmicky quality and for which initial sales may be good but are expected to decline over time. Products that are targeted for special events may also provide initially high returns with a sudden decline following the event. The second case represents MMFs for which revenue projections start off slowly but for which momentum is expected to grow.

Some of these revenue patterns challenge our ability to identify an optimal delivery sequence without succumbing to a brute force calculation of all feasible delivery sequences. IFM pays special attention to MMFs that experience significant increases or decreases in their projected revenues, and when necessary performs additional calculations to determine whether they should be promoted or demoted within the delivery schedule. The following sections describe how this should be accomplished.

Time-Sensitive Delivery

If two organizations are competing to get their product to market first, the one that wins will likely gain a substantial share of the market. This dynamic must be represented in the cost-benefits analysis when such an MMF is being considered during sequencing. Two projections are therefore needed to represent the two significantly different scenarios.

Figure 6.2a illustrates this for an MMF with the monthly costs and revenues as shown. This MMF exhibits a significant reduction in revenue from $40,000 to $30,000 per month if delivered later than the end of the second month. As there are two distinct revenue categories in this example, it is possible to summarize the table according to whether the MMF is delivered in periods 1 to 2 or in periods 3 to 6. This projection summary is shown in Figure 6.2b. The SANPVs are then calculated using the revenue projections appropriate for the given delivery month. For example, the SANPV for period 1 utilizes the early delivery revenue projections, whereas the SANPV for period 3 is calculated using the late delivery revenue projections. The entire set of SANPVs for this MMF are shown in Figure 6.2c. Because two different revenue projections are used to depict early and late delivery options, there is a significant drop in SANPV at period 3.

In fact, what we find is that the previous MMF cost and revenue tables may be over simplistic for those MMFs that exhibit complicated cost and revenue projections. When this occurs, the technique described here and depicted in Figure 6.2 can be used.

Of course deriving revenue projections can be a significant challenge. In many cases they are taken from market surveys and sometimes constructed from rather incomplete knowledge. This is one of the main reasons for

Delivered at End	Monthly Costs and Revenue							
of Month	1	2	3	4	5	6	7	8
1	-60	40	40	40	40	40	40	40
2	n/a	-60	40	40	40	40	40	40
3	n/a	n/a	-60	30	30	30	30	30
4	n/a	n/a	n/a	-60	30	30	30	30
5	n/a	n/a	n/a	n/a	-60	30	30	30
6	n/a	n/a	n/a	n/a	n/a	-60	30	30

a. Revenue Projections according to Development Month

Delivered at End	Monthly Costs and Revenue							
of Month	1	2	3	4	5	6	7	8
1–2 (Early Delivery)	-60	40	40	40	40	40	40	40
3–6 (Late Delivery)	n/a	n/a	-60	30	30	30	30	30

b. Summary of Revenue Projections

	SANPV by Month				
MMF	1	2	3	4	5
A	210	171	84	56	27

c. SANPV Using Early- and Late-delivery Options

Figure 6.2
SANPV for a Time-to-Market Sensitive MMF Using a Discount Rate of 10% per Year ($US in Thousands)

reevaluating the MMF sequencing prior to the start of each MMF. Decisions that previously seemed correct may be challenged by new or more complete information.

The IFM heuristic does not consistently select the optimal delivery sequence when MMFs exhibit these trends. In general, MMFs with critical time-to-market constraints or future exponential growth should be favored early in the schedule, while those that show potential to increase ROI if developed later should be delayed. When these MMFs are present, additional calculations must be performed to compare the delivery sequence identified by the IFM heuristic with one in which the positioning of these timesensitive MMFs is changed.

Exponential Growth Patterns

Sometimes the return from an individual MMF may increase exponentially following delivery. In this case, there is no specific point at which the ROI

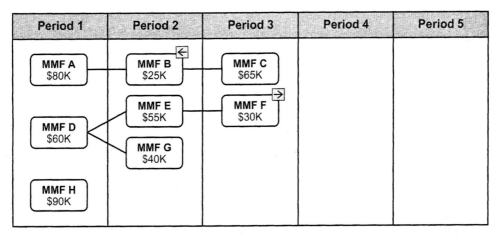

◁ Time sensitive: Must be delivered "early" in the schedule.

▷ Time sensitive: Must be delivered "late" in the schedule.

Figure 6.3
Annotating the MMF Graph with Time Constraints

changes dramatically. When sequencing MMFs, the IFM heuristic assumes relatively stable or slowly increasing revenues. It therefore fails to anticipate the dramatic NPV loss that results from delaying an exponential MMF. Unless this information is considered, the delivery of the MMF could be delayed to a later period without any realization that the anticipated value would not be realized.

Just as we previously annotated the MMF precedence graph to visually identify intangible MMFs, so we can now annotate it to mark MMFs with significant delivery constraints. In Figure 6.3, MMF B should be delivered early in order to fulfill its potential, and MMF F would benefit from later delivery. Once the IFM heuristics have identified the candidate delivery sequence, the NPV from this sequence can be compared to those in which B is promoted and/or F is demoted. These calculations should clearly indicate whether it is worthwhile accommodating the special time-sensitive needs of these MMFs.

Concurrent Development

An alternative or complementary approach to the problem of time-sensitive MMFs is to consider parallel development in which more than one MMF is developed simultaneously. Our examples so far have assumed that only one

MMF will be under development during each period, but in the real world concurrent development of MMFs may be both necessary and desirable. In fact, this sequential simplification not only assumes that the granularity of the periods are small enough to act as a common denominator to all the MMFs in the project, but also implies that MMFs are either distributed in such a way as to keep resource requirements constant or requires resource allocation to be performed at the start of each MMF development iteration. It is unlikely that either of these assumptions holds true in a real-world development project scenario.

It turns out that the IFM heuristic is equally effective for creating concurrent sequences of MMFs as long as the allocation of MMFs to periods occurs during the generation of the sequence. In other words, we cannot assume that the MMF sequence developed for a purely serial schedule can simply be compressed into a shorter number of concurrent periods, as this approach would be unlikely to deliver the maximum NPV. Clearly, an assumption of the IFM heuristic is that selection of the next MMF is for a specific and known period.

Consider the set of MMFs A through E whose costs and revenues are shown in Figure 6.4a along with their precursors in Figure 6.4b. The WSANPVs of the resulting strands are shown in Figure 6.4c. In this table, we have applied a weighting factor of 15% and have assumed that the periods are months and the discount rate is 10% per year. MMFs C and D both require two periods of development. We show this using the notation introduced in Chapter 5, in which additional development periods are represented by periods after the MMF. MMF C is, therefore, represented in its strands as "**C.**" and D as "**D.**"

In a serial development context, and by reference to the table in Figure 6.4c, the IFM heuristic would select MMF D from the strand **D.E** for the first period. Because D requires two periods of development, the next period for consideration is period 3. Examining the WSANPVs for period 3 reveals MMF E to be the winner. Continuing in this manner, the IFM heuristic produces the seven-period sequence **D.EC.AB**.

Using the costs and revenues shown in Figure 6.5, we can compute the cash positions for this sequence and then its discounted cash flow using the techniques described in Chapter 2. This reveals that the selected sequence requires just $80,000 to fund and has a very healthy NPV of $981,000. It becomes self-funding in period 4 and the breakeven time is 7.04 periods (by linear regression). The results are shown in Figure 6.5. Further investigation reveals that there is no other linear sequence that returns greater NPV.

MMF	Periods															
	1	2	3	4	5	6	7	8	9	10	11	12	13	14	15	16
A	-50	10	10	10	10	10	10	10	10	10	10	10	10	10	10	10
B	-20	10	10	9	8	7	6	5	4	3	2	1	0	0	0	0
C	-20	-20	10	13	16	19	22	25	25	25	25	25	25	25	25	25
D	-20	-20	10	14	18	22	26	30	34	38	40	40	40	40	40	40
E	-50	35	35	35	35	35	35	35	35	35	35	35	35	35	35	35

Figure 6.4a
MMF Table (in $US Thousands)

MMF	Precursor
A	
B	A
C	
D	
E	D

Figure 6.4b
Precursor Table

Strand	Periods															
	1	2	3	4	5	6	7	8	9	10	11	12	13	14	15	16
E	439	405	372	338	305	272	239	207	174	142	111	79	48	17	-14	-44
D.	304	271	240	208	177	146	115	86	60	37	17	1	-13	-23	-30	-15
D.E	510	460	411	362	313	264	217	170	127	86	48	13	-20	-50	-25	-12
C.	205	185	165	145	126	106	87	67	48	29	13	-1	-13	-23	-30	-15
A	90	81	71	62	53	44	35	26	17	8	-1	-10	-18	-27	-36	-44
B	42	42	42	41	41	40	38	35	31	27	21	15	8	0	-9	-18
AB	112	104	96	88	79	69	59	48	37	24	12	-2	-16	-31	-45	-37

Figure 6.4c
15% Weighted SANPVs with Discount 0.8% per Period ($US in Thousands)

Because the business only needs to invest $80,000 to fund this project and it receives over $1 million in return, the ROI over 16 periods is exceptionally impressive—1349% by the standard reckoning outlined in Chapter 2.

Now let's reconsider a scenario in which concurrent development of two MMFs is allowed. In this particular example, we assume that it is not possible to accelerate the development of any individual MMF but that additional resources make it possible for more MMFs to be developed concurrently. Again to simplify this example, we also assume that only two MMFs may be under development in each period.

Sequence	MMF	\	\	\	\	\	\	Periods	\	\	\	\	\	\	\	\	\	Net
		1	2	3	4	5	6	7	8	9	10	11	12	13	14	15	16	
D.EC.AB	D	-20	-20	10	14	18	22	26	30	34	38	40	40	40	40	40	40	392
	.																	
	E			-50	35	35	35	35	35	35	35	35	35	35	35	35	35	405
	C				-20	-20	10	13	16	19	22	25	25	25	25	25	25	190
	.																	
	A						-50	10	10	10	10	10	10	10	10	10	10	50
	B							-20	10	10	9	8	7	6	5	4	3	42
Cash		-20	-20	-40	29	33	17	64	101	108	114	118	117	116	115	114	113	1,079
Investment		-20	-20	-40														-80
ROI																		1349%
Self-fund Status					x													
PV		-20	-20	-39	28	32	16	61	95	101	105	108	106	105	103	101	100	981
Rolling NPV		-20	-40	-79	-50	-19	-3	58	153	253	359	467	573	678	781	882	981	
Breakeven Status							x											7.04

Figure 6.5
ROI and Discounted Cash Flow for Serial Sequence ($US in Thousands)

The sequencing task starts off in the same way as the previous example by selecting strand **D**. However this time because two MMFs are allowed per period, a second MMF can also be selected for period 1. On analyzing the remaining strands we find that **E** has an unfulfilled precursor of MMF D and is therefore ineligible for selection. The next most promising strand is **C.**, so this is selected for development. In period 2, MMFs C and D are still under construction. In period 3 the leading candidate is again the strand **E.**. On this occasion we can select it because its precursor, MMF D, has now been scheduled. The next most interesting strand is **AB**, so MMF A is selected. By period 4, the only remaining candidate is **B**, so it is duly selected. Figure 6.6 illustrates the resulting parallel sequence.

In practice, deciding which combination of MMFs to select for the next development period must take into consideration the number and skill sets of the available personnel as well as availability of other resources. A carefully defined specification of the resource requirements for each MMF is therefore necessary prior to scheduling. A full discussion of specific resource allocation models is beyond the scope of this book; however, resource allocation could be as simple as considering story points and team velocity in

Periods			
1	2	3	4
D.		E	B
C.		A	

Figure 6.6
Parallel Sequencing

XP, or could be a much more complex model in which very specific requirements are matched against the skill sets and availability of personnel.

Yet another factor of considerable importance is the impact of concurrent development on the project financing and NPV. Figure 6.7 examines the cash positions and discounted cash flow of our new parallel sequence.

It's informative to compare Figure 6.7 with Figure 6.5, in order to see the impact of concurrent development on some of the major financial metrics. The advantages of parallel development are that the project can be completed in only four periods instead of the initial seven periods. Concurrent development also accelerates the breakeven time from 7.04 to 6.23 periods and increases NPV from $981,000 to $1,083,000. A major trade-off is that the project now requires an initial investment of $160,00 as opposed to $80,000 for the serial sequence.

Not surprisingly, parallel development places a heavier demand on the business for initial funding, and in general, it only marginally increases the NPV of the project. However, the impact on ROI is usually more marked. In this case, ROI has decreased to 742%, mainly because of the higher investment costs. The benefits of parallel development need to be weighed carefully against these results.

As illustrated in this example, IFM provides important information for understanding the impact of parallel development on the project finances and for determining when and where it makes sense to select a parallel delivery option.

Sequence	MMF	1	2	3	4	5	6	7	8	9	10	11	12	13	14	15	16	Net
D.EB	D	-20	-20	10	14	18	22	26	30	34	38	40	40	40	40	40	40	392
	•																	
	E			-50	35	35	35	35	35	35	35	35	35	35	35	35	35	405
	B			-20	10	10	9	8	7	6	5	4	3	2	1	0		45
	•																	
C.A	C	-20	-20	10	13	16	19	22	25	25	25	25	25	25	25	25	25	265
	•																	0
	A			-50	10	10	10	10	10	10	10	10	10	10	10	10		80
Cash		-40	-40	-80	52	89	96	102	108	111	114	115	114	113	112	111	110	1,187
Investment		-40	-40	-80														-160
ROI																		742%
Self-fund Status					x													
PV		-40	-39	-78	50	86	92	96	101	103	105	105	104	102	100	99	97	1,083
Rolling NPV		-40	-79	-157	-107	-21	70	167	268	371	477	582	686	788	888	986	1,083	
Breakeven Status							x											6.23

Figure 6.7
ROI and Discounted Cash Flow of Parallel Sequence ($US in Thousands)

Summary

This chapter discussed several issues related to implementing IFM in a real-world context:

- MMFs come in many different shapes and sizes. Those with specific time-to-market constraints or that exhibit exponential growth may need to be promoted or demoted within the delivery sequence. NPV calculations are performed to test alternate delivery options.

- The delivery of key MMFs can also be accelerated through the use of parallel development. The IFM heuristic can be used to analyze con-current development options and provides visibility into the NPV, ROI, and funding impact of concurrency.

References

1. Brian Nejmeh and Ian Thomas, "Business-Driven Product Planning Using Feature Vectors and Increments," *IEEE Software,* December 2002, Vol. 19, No. 6.

2. Ram Chillarege, "The Marriage of Business Dynamics and Software Engineering," *IEEE Software*, December 2002, Vol. 19, No. 6.

Managing Intangibles

It is widely recognized that intangibles contribute significant value to a project. This chapter describes an approach by which intangibles are evaluated through the use of pairwise comparisons. This enables the IFM heuristic to consider both tangibles and intangibles during the sequencing process and provide metrics that clearly identify the impact of intangibles on the project-level returns.■

Apples and Oranges: Dealing with Intangibles

An intangibly valued MMF is one that has implicit value to the customer but for which the value cannot be easily quantified [1,2,3,4]. Because many project managers consider intangibles to be at least equally important to tangibles, we need to seriously consider their role within IFM and determine how they should be identified, evaluated, prioritized, and ultimately sequenced within the MMF delivery schedule [5].

Consider an example of two small MMFs for an online instructor evaluation form at a university. The MMFs include the following:

- MMF A: Online evaluation system. Students fill in a multiple-choice survey of their instructor's performance at the end of each semester. Scores are tallied and reported to the instructor and administrators.

- MMF B: Comment system. Students write individual comments to their instructor on specific aspects of the course.

The benefits of the first MMF are obvious, and in fact due to the size of the university and the number and diversity of courses offered, the cost of developing the MMF would be recouped within a single semester. These high returns fully justify development of the MMF.

The anticipated returns of the second MMF are less easily quantified. In fact, previous pen and paper efforts to elicit comments from students failed to produce any significant results. The obvious risk is that students will continue their practice of not taking the time to write detailed comments to the instructor, in which case investing time and effort in developing this MMF would be nonproductive. Despite this possibility, the MMF appears enticing. Simply bringing the process online and enabling students to fill in the forms in the privacy of their own homes might produce better results. More importantly, the university wants to know whether the potential value of the MMF is significant enough to validate the risks involved.

The following intangible benefits have been identified:

- Increased quality of feedback between students and instructors, contributing to improved courses
- Increased student satisfaction with their ability to provide feedback

The primary ROI was attributed to the first benefit, because improved course quality will increase student retention and draw new students to the university. Quantifying the extent to which this would occur could, however, be very difficult. The remainder of this chapter discusses how this type of analysis can be accomplished.

Managing Intangibles

We will consider two basic approaches to this problem. The first method does not attempt to quantify ROI for intangibles but simply annotates the precedence graph to indicate the presence of an intangible and to bring it to the attention of developers. The plus sign (+) indicates that an MMF carries significant yet unquantified value. In Figure 7.1, MMFs C and G on the precedence graph are enhanced for intangibles. MMF G is entirely intangible, with no easily quantifiable ROI value. In contrast, MMF C is partially quantifiable (to the tune of $65,000), but carries an additional intangible component.

With this method, the IFM sequencing algorithm orders MMFs solely according to SANPV values, and intangibles are not included. The responsibility of bringing intangible MMFs into the sequence is then placed squarely

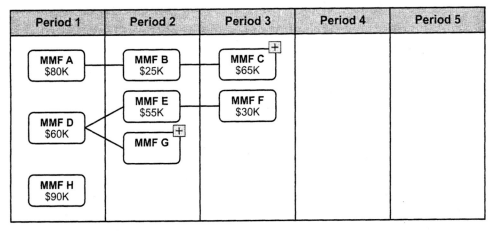

Period 1	Period 2	Period 3	Period 4	Period 5
MMF A $80K	MMF B $25K	MMF C $65K [+]		
	MMF E $55K	MMF F $30K		
MMF D $60K	MMF G [+]			
MMF H $90K				

[+] Intangible benefits

Figure 7.1
Annotating the Precedence Graph with Intangibles

upon the shoulders of the project manager, who must observe and analyze each intangible and determine how it should be scheduled. This approach obviously diminishes the automation power of IFM, and its success is largely dependent on the skill, intuition, and experience of the project manager and developers. This approach does not enhance the goal of IFM to create an ROI-informed development environment and so is not encouraged. However, it has certain appeal because it means that we do not even try to quantify something that has previously been categorized as unquantifiable.

The second method, which is described here in more detail, uses pairwise comparisons to translate intangible benefits into normalized NPV values. Once normalized in this way, all MMFs can be treated uniformly during sequencing, thereby supporting a much higher level of automation. The resulting delivery sequence can then be analyzed to calculate projected NPV with and without intangibles, as well as the lost opportunity costs experienced as a result of scheduling the intangibles. This analysis provides the project manager with very realistic projections of how the project might be expected to perform and enables informed trade-off decisions concerning the inclusion or exclusion of intangibles.

With increased emphasis on continual process improvement, organizations can compare these projections to the actual ROI measured following system delivery. This feedback can enable improved estimates on subsequent projects [6,7].

A Pairwise Approach to Quantifying Intangibles

The analytical hierarchical process (AHP) has been shown to be effective in solving the problem of prioritizing requirements [8,9]. Instead of simply determining the perceived importance of each requirement, the AHP process involves pairwise comparisons between each individual requirement in the set. This is effective because multiple pairwise comparisons are used to evaluate a requirement, and individual errors tend to cancel each other out. The approach is generally accepted to be more reliable than simply ranking each requirement according to its perceived importance.

AHP's underlying concept of using pairwise comparisons can also be applied to the problem of quantifying intangible MMFs. The entire process involves the following steps.

Step 1: Identify a Set of Gauges

IFM uses a comparative process to normalize intangible benefits in terms of NPV equivalencies. This means that an MMF with identified intangible benefits is compared to a series of MMFs with quantified revenue projections. As a result, each intangible MMF is ascribed revenue-equivalent values that can be used to calculate its NPV. Although these values cannot be considered as reliable as the NPVs of tangible MMFs, they are still useful in the sequencing process, and as we will demonstrate later, provide some extremely useful information for estimating critical project characteristics.

In a typical software system certain MMFs will be primarily quantifiable, others will be entirely intangible, and still others will contain both tangible and intangible values.

Consider a system that is decomposed into 10 MMFs, labeled from A to J. Of these, MMFs B, C, D, F, G, H, and I have quantifiable revenue projections; MMFs A and E are intangible; and MMF J contains both tangibles and intangibles. This situation is depicted in Figure 7.2. The revenue projections for intangible MMFs A and E are temporarily replaced with a question mark (?). As MMF J returns both tangible and intangible value the tangible revenues in the MMF table are annotated with a "?" to depict the additional intangible aspect.

To support the process of determining revenue equivalencies for intangible MMFs it is necessary to identify a small subset of tangible MMFs. These MMFs are referred to as "gauges" because they are used for measuring and comparing revenues. To simplify the process further, these MMF gauges must also exhibit typical revenue characteristics, meaning they should not

MMF	Periods							
	1	2	3	4	5	6	7	8
A	-32	?	?	?	?	?	?	?
B	-50	10	14	22	36	52	72	96
C	-85	32	32	32	32	32	32	32
D	-60	20	23	26	30	28	25	22
E	-60	?	?	?	?	?	?	?
F	-120	42	44	46	48	50	52	54
G	-60	40	40	30	20	20	10	10
H	-60	21	22	23	24	25	26	27
I	-50	15	15	15	15	15	15	15
J	-20	15?	15?	15?	15?	15?	15?	15?

Figure 7.2
Costs and revenues for Tangible and Intangible MMFs ($US in Thousands).
Intangible Revenue Is Defined by "?."

exhibit delivery sensitivities or unusual patterns of revenue generation, but should follow a standard curve of projected revenues. The reasoning behind this constraint is explained later, however we should point out that what might be considered standard for one domain or set of circumstances might be atypical for another.

Finally, in order to reduce the number of project-wide comparisons, the set of gauges should be limited to between three and five. Additional gauges can be added as needed. For example, if a particular intangible MMF results in large discrepancies in its evaluated revenue projections, then additional gauges should be added and further comparisons made.

In the example shown in Figure 7.2, MMFs C, F, and H are selected as gauges because all of them behave in a standard way with either the same revenue from period to period or a gradual increase in revenue. Other MMFs such as B and D were rejected for different reasons. For example, MMF B exhibits unusual exponential growth while MMF D exhibits a bell shaped revenue curve. Interestingly, a bell shaped revenue curve might be considered normal if the analysis period were extended over a longer period, however in this example for which analysis extends only 8 quarters, this would be atypical. MMF I could have been selected if an additional gauge were needed, however three gauges were deemed sufficient for the initial analysis. As mentioned previously, the type of revenue curve that might be considered normal is dependent upon many factors including the number and duration of the analysis periods, and the characteristics of the project under development.

Step 2: Construct a Pairwise Comparison Table

Once the gauges are identified, a table is constructed in which each gauge is assigned a column, and its total revenue over the entire analysis period is displayed at the foot of each column. This is calculated by simply summing the MMF's individual revenues for each period within the scope of the analysis. This figure is not used for calculations per se but provides useful information during the pairwise comparison process.

Each of the intangible MMFs, which in this case includes MMFs A and E, are then assigned individual rows in the table. The table for the current example is depicted in Figure 7.3.

Step 3: Make Pairwise Comparisons

Each intangible MMF is now compared to each of the gauges in turn. For each comparison, a value is assigned that captures the relative value of the two MMFs. Figure 7.4 illustrates that in this example, MMF A was assessed at half the value of MMF C, two fifths of the value of MMF F, and two thirds of the of value of MMF H. MMF E was valued more highly at one and a quarter times the value of MMF C, four fifths of MMF F, and one and two thirds the value of MMF H. Of course these results are subjective, but they are based on a detailed analysis of the perceived value of the intangible benefits and standardized to some extent through the redundancy of making several pairwise comparisons.

We need to bear in mind that these figures are derived from informed estimates and should be used accordingly. It would be unwise to base the justification of a project purely on intangibles. However the advantages of this

		Gauges: MMFs with Quantitatively Valued ROI Selected for Comparison Purposes		
MMFs		**C**	**F**	**H**
A				
E				
Total Revenue over Analysis Period		$224	$336	$168

Figure 7.3
A Pairwise Comparison Table

Gauges: MMFs with
Quantitatively Valued ROI Selected
for Comparison Purposes

MMFs	C	F	H
A	0.5	0.4	0.67
E	1.25	0.8	1.67
Total Revenue over Analysis Period	$224	$336	$168

Intangibly Valued MMFs { A, E }

Figure 7.4
Comparing Intangibles against Tangibles

approach are that determining SANPV equivalencies for all MMFs enables delivery sequencing to be automated and provides informative data about the project. For example, it is useful to be able to distinguish between tangibles and intangibles in the cost-benefit analysis, and to explore alternate delivery sequences and potential NPV of projects that exclude intangibles from development. These ideas are explored later in more depth.

Step 4: Calculate Equivalent SANPVs

In order to calculate equivalent NPV values we should first observe that it is the revenue of each MMF that is compared and not its costs. In fact, MMF costs are just as easily calculated for intangibles as they are for tangibles. The SANPV calculations should therefore use the known costs for each intangible in conjunction with the revenues determined through the pairwise comparison process. The next step is therefore to calculate these equivalent NPV values.

As depicted in Figure 7.5, an individual table is constructed for each of the intangible MMFs (A and E). Figure 7.5a shows the costs and revenues of the MMF gauges. Revenue calculations for MMF A are shown in Figure 7.5b and for MMF E in Figure 7.5c. In this example we focus on MMF A. The cost of developing MMF A is projected at $32,000 and is initially shown within period 1. Additional rows are then created for comparing MMF A against the gauges MMFs C, F, and H. The previously determined ratios of 0.5, 0.4, and 0.67 are also shown in their respective rows. The remainder of the table is then easily calculated by multiplying the corresponding ratios against the revenue projection values shown in Figure 7.5a. For example, the A vs. F row

Tangible MMFs	1	2	3	4	5	6	7	8
MMF C	-85	32	32	32	32	32	32	32
MMF F	-120	42	44	46	48	50	52	54
MMF H	-60	21	22	23	24	25	26	27

a. Costs and Revenues for MMF Gauges

Comparisons for Intangible MMF A		1	2	3	4	5	6	7	8
A vs. C	0.5		16.0	16.0	16.0	16.0	16.0	16.0	16.0
A vs. F	0.4	-32	16.8	17.6	18.4	19.2	20.0	20.8	21.6
A vs. H	0.67		14.0	15.0	15.0	16.0	17.0	17.0	18.0
Synthesized Returns for MMF A			15.6	16.1	16.6	17.1	17.6	18.1	18.6

b. Calculating Revenue Equivalencies for Intangible MMF A

Comparisons for Intangible MMF E		1	2	3	4	5	6	7	8
E vs. C	1.25		40.0	40.0	40.0	40.0	40.0	40.0	40.0
E vs. F	0.8	-60	33.6	35.2	36.8	38.4	40.0	41.6	43.2
E vs. H	1.67		35.1	36.7	38.4	40.1	41.8	43.4	45.1
Synthesized Returns for MMF E			36.2	37.3	38.4	39.5	40.6	41.7	42.8

c. Calculating Revenue Equivalencies for Intangible MMF E

Figure 7.5
Step-by-Step Calculation of Revenues for Intangible MMFs ($US in Thousands, Rounded to the Nearest $100)

period 2 figure is calculated as revenue *(C, period 2)* × ratio (A vs. F), which calculates as $42,000 × 0.4 = $16,800. Each remaining cell in Figures 7.5b and 7.5c is similarly calculated. Revenue calculations start at period 2, because even in the earliest delivery option, period 1 would be used for development.

The next step involves calculating the average equivalent revenue values for each intangible MMF. This is a simple calculation that averages all of the results from the pairwise calculations to determine equivalent revenues.

The second period revenue for MMF A is therefore calculated as

$$((\$32,000 \times 0.5) + (\$42,000 \times 0.4) + (\$1,000 \times 0.67))/3 =$$
$$(\$16,000 + \$16,800 + \$14,000) /3 = \$15,600$$

This figure appears in the bottom row of Figure 7.5b under period 2. The remaining figures in that row are similarly calculated, resulting in a synthesized set of returns for intangible MMF A. A similar process is followed in Figure 7.5c to determine the revenues for intangible MMF E.

Hybrid MMFs

Finally we need to consider MMF J, which returns both tangible and intangible value. There are a couple of options for calculating revenues for such hybrid MMFs. The first option is to apply a pairwise comparison with the set of MMF gauges. Another option is simply to apply a multiplier to the tangible revenue. The first option is more favorable when an MMF is primarily intangible, and the second one when the MMF is primarily tangible. In this case, it is determined that MMF J is primarily tangible and that intangibles add an additional 25% to its value. The revenues for MMF J are therefore multiplied by 1.25 to obtain full revenue projections.

Now that we have numerical values for the intangible and hybrid MMFs we can create SANPV values for them using the same approach described for tangible MMFs in Chapter 5. Figure 7.6 shows the results of the calculation, assuming our previous adopted discount rate of 10% per year, equivalent to 2.4% per quarterly period.

The Impact of Intangibles on the Cost-Benefits Analysis

From a business perspective, it is important to understand the impact of intangibles on the revenue projections of the project. IFM provides this type of information to the business stakeholders. Figure 7.7 identifies several critical project-level factors, including baseline projections obtained from tangible MMFs only, potential revenues obtained from both tangibles and intangibles, alternate delivery options, and potential lost opportunity costs. These are each discussed in more detail in the following sections.

MMF	Periods							
	1	2	3	4	5	6	7	8
A	75	58	42	27	12	-1	-14	-26
E	187	148	110	75	41	9	-21	-50
J	97	80	63	46	30	14	-1	-17

Figure 7.6
SANPVs for Intangible & Hybrid MMFs at Discount Rate 2.4% / Period ($US in Thousands)

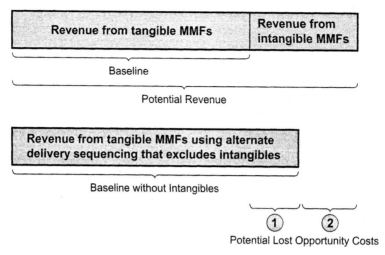

Figure 7.7
IFM Informed Approach to Intangibles

As a result of the analysis of intangible MMFs undertaken above, we can complete the cost-benefits analysis for both tangible and intangible MMFs. Figure 7.8 shows a complete SANPV table for all MMFs, tangible and intangible. These SANPV figures are now used to illustrate the following project-level metrics.

Imagine that the following delivery sequence has been selected: B and E in period 1, F and C in period 2, G and J in period 3, I and D in period 4, and A and H in period 5.

MMF	Periods							
	1	2	3	4	5	6	7	8
A	75	58	42	27	12	-1	-14	-26
B	211	129	67	24	-6	-23	-34	-41
C	116	88	60	32	6	-20	-45	-70
D	96	76	54	30	5	-16	-34	-50
E	186	148	110	75	41	9	-21	-50
F	180	132	87	45	5	-32	-67	-99
G	96	86	75	58	40	15	-18	-50
H	90	66	44	22	3	-16	-33	-50
I	44	31	18	6	-6	-18	-30	-41
J	97	80	63	46	30	14	-1	-17

Figure 7.8
SANPV Table for Both Tangible and Intangible MMFs at 2.4% / Period ($US in Thousands)

There are three calculations of specific interest that together provide a very clear picture of predicted ROI as well as the possible lost opportunity costs of developing intangible MMFs instead of more tangible ones.

Baseline NPV

The baseline calculation excludes intangible MMFs. It sums the NPVs of only the tangible MMFs and therefore represents the base-level NPV of the project before intangibles are introduced. It is calculated by summing all tangible MMFs including the part of MMF J that was considered tangible.

If the notation SANPV(M,P) represents the NPV of MMF M when its development begins in period P, then

$$
\begin{aligned}
\text{NPV}_{\text{baseline}} &= \text{SANPV(B,1)} + \text{SANPV(F,2)} + \text{SANPV(C,2)} + \\
&\quad \text{SANPV(G,3)} + (\text{SANPV(J,3)}/1.25) + \text{SANPV(1,4)} + \\
&\quad \text{SANPV(D,4)} + \text{SANPV(H,5)} \\
\\
&= \$211{,}000 + \$132{,}000 + \$88{,}000 + \$75{,}000 + \\
&\quad (\$63{,}000)/1.25 + \$33{,}000 + \$30{,}000 + \$3{,}000 \\
\\
&= \$622{,}000
\end{aligned}
$$

Potential NPV

The potential NPV calculation incorporates the equivalent SANPVs of the intangible MMFs into the calculation. Potential NPV therefore reflects a more optimistic view of the project assuming the intangibles do indeed deliver as predicted.

$$
\begin{aligned}
\text{NPV}_{\text{potential}} &= \text{SANPV(B,1)} + \text{SANPV(E,1)} + \text{SANPV(F,2)} + \\
&\quad \text{SANPV(C,2)} + \text{SANPV(G,3)} + \text{SANPV(J,3)} + \\
&\quad \text{SANPV(1,4)} + \text{SANPV(D,4)} + \text{SANPV(A,5)} + \text{SANPV(H,5)} \\
\\
&= \$211{,}000 + \$186{,}000 + \$132{,}000 + \$88{,}000 + \$75{,}000 + \\
&\quad \$63{,}000 + \$33{,}000 + \$30{,}000 + \$12{,}000 + \$3{,}000 \\
\\
&= \$833{,}000
\end{aligned}
$$

This metric provides a more complete picture of the value of the project by incorporating the perceived value of intangibles.

Lost Opportunity Costs

The previous calculations provide an upper and lower bound on the predicted NPV (risks aside), but in both cases the intangible MMFs were scheduled as part of the delivery sequence.

However, lost opportunity costs should also be considered. Lost opportunity costs represent losses that might occur as a result of taking a certain course of action. Figure 7.7 identifies two distinct lost opportunity costs, marked ① and ② on the diagram.

In case ①, an alternate MMF delivery schedule is proposed that excludes the sequencing of intangibles. In other words, NPV is optimized for tangible (quantifiable) MMFs only. We choose to include the hybrid MMF J because it is primarily a tangible MMF. In this example, the same set of MMFs without intangibles would be optimized by the delivery sequence of B and F in period 1, G and C in period 2, J and D in period 3, and H and I in period 4, which translates to the following ROI calculation:

$$NPV_{\text{optimized for tangibles}} = SANPV(B,1) + SANPV(F,1) + SANPV(C,2) +$$
$$SANPV(G2) + SANPV(J,3) + SANPV(D,3) +$$
$$SANPV(I,4) + SANPV(H,4)$$

$$= \$211{,}000 + \$180{,}000 + \$88{,}000 + \$86{,}000 + \$63{,}000 + \\ \$54{,}000 + \$33{,}000 + \$22{,}000$$

$$= \$737{,}000$$

By comparing this value with the NPV_{baseline} value, it is possible to calculate the lost opportunity cost of incorporating the intangible MMFs in the delivery sequence as opposed to focusing entirely on more tangible ones.

$$\text{Lost opportunity cost} = NPV_{\text{optimized for tangibles}} - NPV_{\text{baseline}}$$

$$= \$737{,}000 - \$622{,}000$$

$$= \$115{,}000$$

This figure represents the specific investment risk of developing the intangible MMFs. Of course, if project managers decide not to develop the intangible MMFs, then a matching, albeit slightly riskier, lost opportunity cost represents the loss in potential revenue generation from the intangible assets. This cost is marked in Figure 7.7 as ②, and is calculated as

$$\text{Lost opportunity cost} = NPV_{\text{potential}} - NPV_{\text{optimized for tangibles}}$$

$$= \$833{,}000 - \$737{,}000$$

$$= \$96{,}000$$

As we stated earlier, IFM is not so much an ROI-driven approach as an ROI-informed one. These calculations enable project managers and developers to make informed decisions about the returns and lost opportunities of various development options.

Summary

This chapter lays out the case for incorporating intangibles into the cost-benefits analysis of a project. However, because intangibles are by nature unquantifiable, even pairwise comparisons fall short in identifying the intangible benefits of an MMF.

IFM provides sound financial analysis of a project by considering the impact of intangibles on the baseline and the potential revenues. By instituting a continuous process improvement into an organization, we can improve the accuracy of projections for both tangible and intangible features.

This chapter covered the following points:

- Many project managers consider intangibles to be a critical factor in a project.
- Intangibles can be handled manually by annotating the MMF precedence graph. However, this approach diminishes opportunities for automation and relies primarily on individual skills and intuition of the project manager.
- An alternate approach involves the use of pairwise comparisons between intangibles and tangibles to determine comparative SANPV values for the intangibles.
- Pairwise comparisons build redundancy into the process, which results in a more accurate estimation of overall project NPV than if SANPV equivalencies were directly assigned to the intangible MMFs.
- Project-level metrics distinguish between baseline NPV and the larger potential NPV that arises from considering intangibles.
- Alternate delivery options that exclude intangibles can be explored.
- IFM analysis enables developers and managers to make informed decisions about the trade-offs of tangibles and intangibles within a project.

References

1. J. King and E. Schrems, "Cost-Benefit Analysis in Information Systems Development and Operation," *ACM Computing Surveys*, 10(1): March 1978.

2. P. Sassone, "Cost-Benefit Analysis of Information Systems: A Survey of Methodologies," ACM / IEEE Conference on Supporting Group Work, Palo Alto, California, 1988, pp. 126–133.

3. E. Brynjolfsson and S. Yang, "The Intangible Benefits and Costs of Investments: Evidence from Financial Markets," Proceedings of the 18th International Conference on Information Systems, Atlanta, Georgia, 1997, pp. 147–166.

4. L. Smith and A. Steadman, "Gaining Confidence in Using Return on Investment and Earned Value," *Crosstalk Magazine*, April 1999. Available online at http://www.stsc.hill.af.mil/crosstalk

5. P. Klein, "Rationalize This! ROI Strategies Abound," *Information Week*, August 6, 2001. Available online at http://www.informationweek.com

6. T. Olson, N. Reizer, and J. Over, "A Software Process Framework for the Capability Maturity Model," *Technical Report, Software Engineering Institute,* Carnegie Mellon University. Available online at http://www.sei.cmu.edu

7. W. Humphreys, *Managing the Software Process,* Reading, Massachusetts: Addison Wesley, 1989.

8. Joachim Karlsson and Kevin Ryan, "A Cost-Value Approach for Prioritizing Requirements," *IEEE Software*, 14 (5): 67–74, 1997.

9. T. L. Saaty, *Fundamentals of Decision Making and Priority Theory*, 2nd ed. Pittsburgh, Pennsylvania: RWS Publications, 2000.

IFM and the Unified Process

8

Incremental funding strategies enhance the unified process by providing business-level support. During early phases, requirements are grouped into customer-valued features, which are then delivered incrementally throughout the remainder of the project. The delivery sequence is arranged to optimize NPV and identify strategies for obtaining early self-funding of a project. ■

Introduction

This chapter describes the implementation of incremental funding strategies within the rational Unified process (RUP) [1,2]. On its journey from inception to completion, a software application passes through several distinct phases. Each phase defines the primary engineering activities and the amount of each activity that should be occurring at that stage of the project. The transitions from one phase to the next are guarded by milestones, or "phase gates," that act as go/no-go decision points. At each of these the stakeholders decide whether to proceed to the next phase. These phases and milestones are used to manage the growth of the software application and to ensure it progresses efficiently toward its final goal.

Technically IFM can be applied within the standard four RUP phases, with more emphasis on inception and elaboration during the early parts of the project, and greater emphasis on construction and transition during the later iterations of MMF development. However, IFM can be more accurately

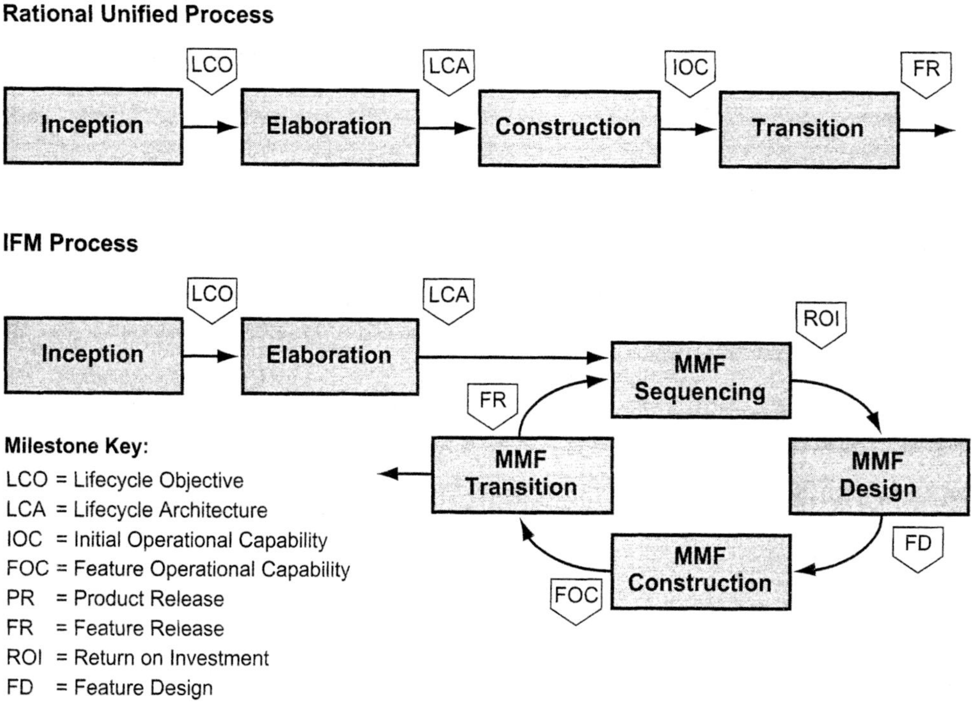

Rational Unified Process

IFM Process

Milestone Key:
LCO = Lifecycle Objective
LCA = Lifecycle Architecture
IOC = Initial Operational Capability
FOC = Feature Operational Capability
PR = Product Release
FR = Feature Release
ROI = Return on Investment
FD = Feature Design

Figure 8.1
Phases of IFM Compared to the Traditional RUP Phases

depicted by the six phases shown in Figure 8.1 of inception, elaboration, MMF sequencing, MMF design, MMF construction, and MMF transition. The inception and elaboration phases are executed at the project level and conducted once at the start of each project. They are only revisited when the design of an MMF challenges the existing architecture or when subsequent versions of the application are being considered. In contrast, the four MMF-related phases of sequencing, design, construction, and transition are executed iteratively.

RUP is an example of the spiral model [3,4], which has been used successfully by many organizations in hundreds of thousands of software projects. Its success is attributed primarily to the fact that it embraces change by revisiting, in each iteration, the major activities such as planning, analysis, development, and stakeholder review. This has the effect of mitigating risk early in the process. Unlike the sequential approach of the waterfall model, spiral projects support concurrent development of artifacts, meaning that analysis, coding, and testing could all occur in the same cycle and continue on into subsequent cycles. Instead of specifying a complete set of requirements at the start of the project, an initial set of requirements can be used to drive the early, high-level architectural design. This facilitates the early identification of risks, and increases the likelihood of delivering a product on time and within budget.

As a spiral project is "grown" it progresses from a set of high-level requirements, candidate architectures, and initial prototypes to a fully developed system delivering all the features specified by the customer. Each of the six IFM phases is composed of one or more smaller spiral iterations that progressively deliver a more complete product. In a typical RUP project, development moves toward delivering the total product to the customer during a single transition phase. In contrast, IFM leads to the development of MMFs that are individually transitioned to the customer. The ordering of MMF development and delivery is planned to maximize ROI by supporting the early generation of revenue from the delivered parts of the system. This chapter describes the phases and milestones from which IFM is composed.

Inception

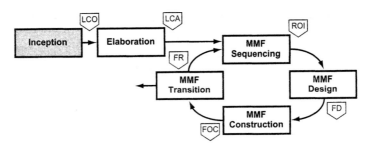

The inception phase primarily focuses on defining the vision and business case for the proposed software product. The vision acts as a driving and unifying force throughout the development process, while the business case provides a rationale for the creation of the product. During this phase, customer involvement is crucial to identifying and negotiating the scope of the project. Often stakeholders will approach the start of a project with diverse ideas and agendas about how the new system should be shaped, and it takes hard work and a commitment to the common good to integrate these divergent goals to achieve a shared vision statement.

Once the vision and business case have been defined, customers identify the major MMFs of the system. As described earlier, an MMF represents a distinct chunk of the system that will return clearly identifiable value. At a later stage in development, the MMFs become the building blocks for reasoning about development and delivery sequencing and for deciding how to maximize the project's value. Once MMFs have been defined, they can be further decomposed into the high-level use cases of the system. In some cases, however, there will be a one-to-one match between an MMF and a use case.

Define the Vision Statement

The vision statement defines the scope of the project and the context in which it will operate. It provides a set of high-level requirements, major constraints, and key features of the system.

To accomplish this, a group of stakeholders are carefully selected to represent the viewpoints and needs of all major project participants. Typically this group includes a balance of users, developers, managers, marketers, and financiers. IFM is a customer-oriented approach, in which customer involvement is seen as a crucial investment from the start of the project, and a broad spectrum of stakeholders is involved at critical stages throughout the process.

Define the Business Case

The business case clearly defines the project context, financial forecast, and success criteria, stated in terms of revenue projections, anticipated savings, enhanced customer loyalty, and so on.

Defining a clear business case is crucial to the success of a software project. Without it, a project will be unlikely to gain sufficient executive support to succeed. This is illustrated by a case study of the State of California's Driver License project, discussed in the 1995 *Chaos Report* [5]. The project, which was started in 1987 to revamp the entire driver's license management process, was finally abandoned $45 million and six years later! The study identified the major cause of this failure as lack of executive buy-in due to an inadequately conceived business case that returned no clear monetary value.

IFM forces the project team to answer critical questions concerning the expected ROI prior to any actual development work. It uses the business case as a context in which to make realistic predictions.

Elicit MMFs

An MMF is defined as the smallest deliverable feature that provides market value in terms of competitive differentiation, source of revenue, cost savings,

MMF	Description	Justification
A.	Flight planner	Increased sales/Office savings
B.	Online calendar	Customer loyalty
C.	Vacation planner	Increased sales/Office savings
D.	Local activities planner	Customer loyalty/Office savings
E.	Tour group organizer	Increased sales/Office savings
F.	Vacation packages	Increased sales/Office savings
G.	Car rental	Revenue from rental companies
H.	Hotel reservation	Revenue from hotels
I.	Online payment	Office savings

Figure 8.2
MMFs for an Online Travel Agency

enhancement of brand projection, or increased customer loyalty. Identifying MMFs is primarily a business-driven activity and as such is the responsibility of the customer or domain experts, with critical input taken from the architects and designers. Experience has shown that in many software applications this activity can be quite intuitive. For example, the identified MMFs for an online vacation service were identified through top-down decomposition and are listed in Figure 8.2. During this phase, each MMF is justified in terms of revenue, cost savings, or some other value creation potential.

Decompose MMFs into Use Cases

MMFs should be further decomposed into the high-level use cases. Use cases define the major functionality of the system, drive the definition of major system requirements, and play a huge role in determining critical system trade-offs.

Drawing from the example of the online travel agency, several of the MMFs could be decomposed into high-level use cases. For example, the MMF labeled "local activities planner," is decomposed in Figure 8.3 into the three use cases of "research local sightseeing information," "book a local tour," and "research local weather conditions." In contrast, the MMF labeled "vacation planner" is not decomposed further at this time.

The decision as to whether a particular MMF should be decomposed into multiple use cases depends on the content of the MMF and the software development practices of the organization. The only stipulation of IFM is that the use cases should be sufficiently decomposed as to support initial cost and effort estimations, and that those figures can be subjected to a meaningful risk analysis.

MMF	Description	Justification
A.	Flight planner	Find a round-trip flight
		Book a flight
		Find a multiple-destination flight
B.	Online calendar	Use calendar-based planner
C.	Vacation planner	Organize vacation
D.	Local activities planner	Research local sightseeing info
		Book a local tour
		Research local weather conditions
E.	Tour group organizer	Organize a group tour
		Manage tour reservations
F.	Vacation packages	Select a vacation package
		Put together a vacation package
G.	Car rental	Rent a car
		Compare rental costs
H.	Hotel reservation	Search for a hotel
		Make a reservation
I.	Online payment	Make a payment

Figure 8.3
Grouping Use Cases

Construct an MMF Graph

MMFs are then formed into a precedence graph, reflecting business, technical, and architectural dependencies. As an example of a business dependency, consider the MMFs "tour group organizer" and "flight planner." From a business perspective it may not make sense to deliver the "tour group organizer" prior to the "flight planner," because the flight planner is needed in order to organize the tour. These are business decisions that are driven by an understanding of the business domain in which the software will operate.

Later, during the MMF sequencing stage, the MMF graph will provide a context for reasoning about the ordering and selection of MMFs within a project timeline. It should be pointed out that the MMF graph represents only a first attempt at identifying dependencies between MMFs at this stage. Many architectural dependencies have yet to be unearthed.

Identify Major Risks Associated with Each MMF

The inception phase must include a high-level risk analysis of the system. During inception, risk analysis focuses primarily on business aspects, but other identified risks related to technology or project factors may also be unearthed. IFM takes a neutral stance with respect to techniques for risk analysis. The business is free to implement whichever techniques are favored or thought appropriate. IFM merely requires that the computed risks be represented in the MMF numbers. However, two primary categories of risk should be examined.

The first category is the business risk that this MMF will or will not be needed. This type of risk analysis is crucial in today's fast-paced business environment in which market demands can change almost overnight and software that is clearly useful today may not be as attractive in the future. One approach to identifying such risks is to compute a probability known as the likelihood factor for each MMF and to multiply projected MMF returns by that factor. For example, an MMF that will definitely be developed is assigned a probability factor of 1, while an MMF with a 50% chance of being developed is assigned 0.5, and so on.

A second category of risk relates to the ability to develop a given MMF. These risks are more dependent on project-level factors such as availability of skilled personnel, buy-in from upper management, complexity of the MMF, and availability of stable tools and platforms. These risks are harder to predict at an early stage because more detailed knowledge of the MMF is needed. During inception, a high-level analysis of such risks is made in order to determine whether the project is even feasible.

Develop a Project Glossary

Finally, in order to synchronize the vocabulary of developer and customer, it is important to develop a project glossary. Although this may at first appear tedious, the rigor of developing a glossary is essential to ensuring that genuine understanding exists. The concept of a glossary is applied in numerous development methodologies, but it is particularly important in IFM because the customer plays such a key part in the decision-making processes.

The Lifecycle Objective Milestone

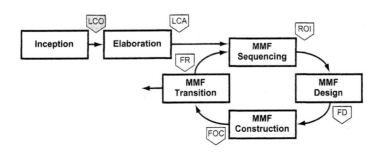

The lifecycle objective (LCO) milestone establishes a transition point between inception and elaboration. One of the primary roles of the LCO is to ensure that risk factors have been adequately addressed and to decide whether the project is viable. In IFM, this is not necessarily a binary decision. The MMF graph usually offers a range of options, the selection of which is supported by IFM financial analysis such as the SANPVs of each MMF. One of the major strengths of IFM is its ability to support reasoning and decision making about which parts of a project make sense to pursue.

Before transitioning to the next phase, stakeholders should therefore agree on initial MMFs and use case definitions, provide rough cost estimates, and undertake risk analysis for each MMF. With this information a consensus can be reached about the feasible scope of the project. In fact, it is quite permissible to identify just one viable MMF that warrants further development and leave other decisions pending.

Elaboration

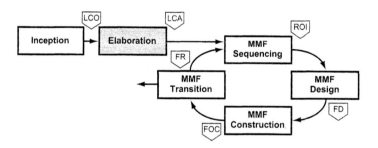

In a traditional RUP project, the architecture is defined up front and often developed as an infrastructure within which the remainder of the application is constructed. In contrast, IFM defines candidate architectures up front but delivers architecture in small increments as needed by individual MMFs. This approach provides the benefits of an overall design without the excessive costs and risks involved in its early construction.

Architectural Selection

During elaboration, several candidate architectures are identified and evaluated against those MMFs that look most promising in terms of value. Whenever possible, IFM promotes the use of proven architectural frameworks. The primary reason for this is that a tried and trusted framework incorporates knowledge and experience gained from countless other software applications. The strengths and weaknesses of each framework are well known, and it is possible to commit to a certain architecture without fully prototyping it in the current project.

Within the RUP context it is also important to take a holistic approach to architecture, because systems should be designed not just for the functional requirements, but also for the nonfunctional ones. These include system qualities, or "ilities," such as scalability, security, manageability, and reliability.

Rather than considering only one architectural solution, it is important to select and evaluate several candidate architectures. There are several approaches that can be used, including the architecture trade-off analysis method (ATAM) [6], which evaluates how well each architecture performs in terms of systemwide nonfunctional requirements. Architectures can then be weighted according to their ability to support the system use cases, and a single architecture selected for the project. Only those MMFs that after SANPV analysis demonstrate real value should be used to define the architecture. MMFs with minimal or zero value need not be considered, since they're unlikely to contribute to the financial success of the project and may not even be selected for sequencing by the IFM heuristic. This additional fine-tuning of architectural options from the perspective of feature value is another expression of the IFM ROI-informed approach to application development.

Once an architecture has been selected, IFM takes the unique step of decomposing it into its primitive elements. For example, a Web-based e-commerce architecture capable of supporting the online travel agency might be decomposed into elements such as Web and application servers, soap clients, an XML parser, and a Web browser. Mid-level design patterns from the architectural framework can also be decomposed into AEs. These primitive elements are then formed into a simple checklist attached to each MMF. The MMF is then evaluated to determine which elements of the architecture must be present in order for the MMF to be implemented. Certain architectural elements may be assigned to several individual MMFs and will be delivered as part of the first MMF to be developed.

Cost and Effort Estimation

Each MMF is then carefully analyzed to determine the cost and effort required to develop it, and in order to predict its projected returns. The high-level use cases may be further decomposed to more clearly specify the required functionality. The NPV prediction is made over a predefined number of time periods and may be sensitive to the delivery date of the MMF. For example, if the customer is interested in NPV over five time periods, the impact of delivering the MMF during each of these time periods must be determined. This determination is critical to the financial sequencing of MMFs, because it is all too common that time-to-market plays a critical role in maximizing potential ROI.

The Lifecycle Architecture Milestone

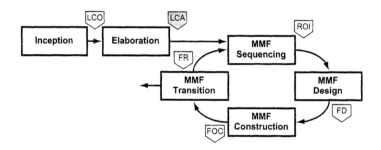

To transition from the architecture phase into the feature delivery phase it is necessary to pass the lifecycle architecture (LCA) milestone. One of the primary roles of the LCA is to assess the level at which the architecture supports the various MMFs. In IFM, this means evaluating whether the selected architecture can support all MMFs at or above a specified NPV threshold, and whether the architecture has been effectively decomposed into more primitive elements and correctly distributed to each MMF.

When IFM is implemented within the unified process, time and effort is invested up front to select an architecture that supports identified MMFs in understandable ways. This could mean that the architecture has the capability of supporting all identified MMFs. On the other hand, it could mean that the architecture easily supports only a few of the more valuable MMFs and would need to be refactored if and when other, less likely MMFs are selected for implementation. IFM enables stakeholders to get involved in the decision-making process and enables them to make informed decisions and trade-offs.

To pass through the LCA milestone, all major stakeholders need to understand the strengths and weaknesses of the selected architecture, including its impact on implementing each of the identified MMFs. AEs must be defined and their costs specified. The stakeholders may also benefit from an initial application of the IFM heuristic to identify a candidate delivery sequence, including all AEs, and the projected funding cost (maximum debt) and breakeven time of the project.

MMF Development and Delivery

The final phases in IFM encompass the actual sequencing, design, development, and transitioning of MMFs. At this point, the initial scope of the project has been clearly defined, and MMFs and AEs have been identified. However, IFM does not lock developers into early project decisions. It embraces change through the iterative nature of the development process, revisiting earlier decisions as necessary throughout the project lifecycle.

The heart and soul of IFM is in the sequencing phase. Inception and elaboration phases pave the way for systematically considering and evaluating various sequencing options. However, it is during the sequencing phase that the actual NPV calculations are performed and the next MMF is selected.

MMF Sequencing

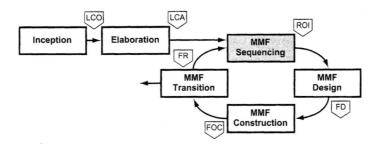

The MMF precedence graph defines the dependencies between IFM elements (MMFs and AEs). Any element with no precursors can potentially be selected as the next one to be developed. Element selection is made by the IFM heuristic.

IFM applies the heuristic described in Chapter 5 to identify not just the next MMF but the entire development schedule. The delivery sequence can be revisited at the start of each MMF iteration in order to update risk-analysis factors or alternations to predicted cost and revenue (both of which lead to modified MMF tables). Reapplying the IFM heuristic to the modified numbers determines whether the sequence should be adjusted.

Depending on available resources and target release dates, it may be beneficial to develop MMFs concurrently, either by starting more than one MMF at the same time or by staggering the start times of overlapping MMFs. Parallel development can occur when MMFs are sufficiently isolated from each other and when interfaces between them are clearly defined up front. This area is covered in Chapter 6. Sufficient staffing must obviously be available to support such parallel activities

NPV Milestone

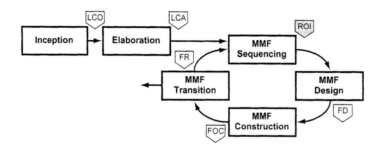

Once sequencing has been completed, we proceed with the current design and construction iteration, which may be for an MMF or an AE.

If no delivery sequences are identified, then development should be suspended until business or other factors change sufficiently to improve the projected returns.

MMF Design

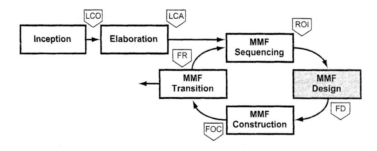

This phase involves the creation of a detailed design for the current MMF or AE. The design is implemented within the constraints of the selected architecture.

Elicit Requirements

Eliciting requirements involves identifying a second tier of stakeholders with specific knowledge and interest in the MMF under development. Whereas the initial set of high-level stakeholders are responsible for shaping and ordering the overall project, these new stakeholders are responsible for defining the more detailed behavior required by the MMF under development. The stakeholders must represent all of the legitimate needs and viewpoints of people affected by the MMF.

Barry Boehm and his colleagues applied the well-known "Theory–W" to develop an extremely effective approach to stakeholder participation and requirements negotiation [7,8]. In this win-win approach, stakeholders take responsibility for identifying and resolving trade-offs between conflicting requirements. By thoroughly investigating options and constraints related to each stakeholder's win conditions, it is possible to reach consensus on a set of requirements, providing beneficial solutions to all.

Using a variety of standard elicitation techniques, stakeholders develop a wish list of features they would like to see in the MMF. The wish list is then developed into a clear and complete set of requirements, which are modeled using use cases. Conflicts are identified and negotiated, possibly using win-win negotiation methods.

Although an initial set of nonfunctional requirements (NFRs) have been elicited earlier in the architectural phase, this activity must now be revisited in light of the specific MMF under consideration. NFRs address a broad array of system characteristics, including performance, security, fault tolerance, portability, and reusability. To minimize risk, these NFRs should be re-evaluated against the selected architecture.

Design

Once the requirements have been identified, the MMF or AE must be designed in more detail. IFM does not dictate a specific design method that should be used. Any use case–driven approach should work well, including a standard object-oriented method, an agile method such as eXtreme programming, or a hybrid approach such as function class decomposition.

MMF Project Plan

A mini-plan is needed to manage the MMF or AE development. This plan addresses issues such as staffing, scheduling, and milestones. If an agile method is used to develop the MMF or AE, this project plan and the following phases would effectively be replaced with the agile development practices.

Feature Design Milestone

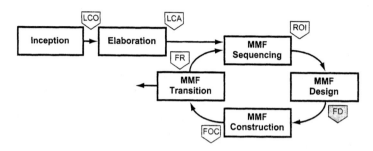

The feature design (FD) milestone provides a concrete checkpoint for determining whether the design for the current IFM element is viable and for validating that all requirements have been elicited and implemented within the design. The checkpoint also serves to validate whether all necessary architectural components needed by this element have been identified.

MMF Construction

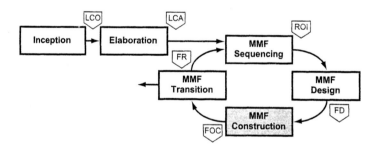

Construction of an MMF or AE involves the instantiation, functional testing, and integration testing of this element.

The remainder of the construction phase focuses on the functionality of the MMF or AE itself. IFM does not prescribe any particular approach to development; however, construction should involve coding, unit testing, and integration testing.

It is important to provide sufficient permanent documentation to support future change management activities, including the design and construction of other MMFs or AEs. Documentation must therefore include at least the following documents:

- Interface documents showing the interface of this element to the rest of the system

- Design documents that have been carefully selected to support ongoing maintenance activities

- Requirements traceability documents identifying critical relationships between requirements, design, implemented code, and performance models

Feature Operational Capability

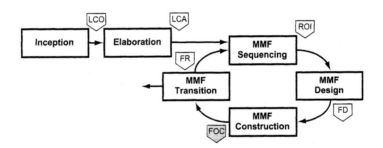

The transition phase primarily involves transferring the MMF or AE from the development stage into the hands of the customer. In the traditional RUP terminology, the initial operational capability (IOC) milestone must be passed before this new phase can be entered. IOC answers questions about the readiness of an application to be deployed into the user community. In IFM, IOC is replaced with feature operational capability (FOC).

With a highly iterative approach such as IFM, in which frequent releases are made to the user, it is even more important that a smooth transition of each IFM element is ensured. The last thing we want is for the users to dread the next release because of all the extra hassle they know it will cause them.

MMF or AE release therefore involves a rigorous metrics-driven testing process in which the MMF or AE is only transitioned to the user once a pre-specified quality has been met. In IFM, the single IOC milestone is replaced with a smaller decision point for each element, the FOC. At this milestone the stakeholders must determine whether the current MMF is ready for release.

MMF Transition

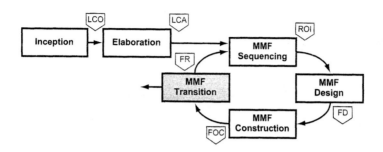

In a typical RUP project, the transition phase can take several iterations, as the project is prepared to be handed over to the client. Transition typically includes activities such as beta testing, conversion of the operation database, user training, performance fine-tuning, and cut-over. In IFM, transition occurs as part of the generation of each IFM element. This has two major implications. First, transition occurs more frequently and each transition contains clearly identified, market-valued functionality. Secondly, apart from the first MMF or AE, elements are transitioned into an already functioning system. In this situation element transition typically will occur as one iteration and will involve working closely with existing users.

Feature Release Milestone

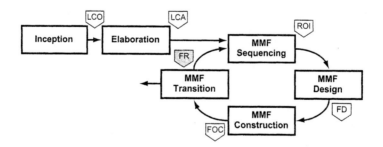

Following the transition stage, a final milestone known as feature release is implemented to determine when the release has been successfully accomplished and to act as a specific milestone between transition and maintenance phases.

This milestone can also provide the opportunity for evaluating the successes and failures of the current iteration. Metrics captured during the iteration can be evaluated to determine the success of various activities, and processes and activities can be changed to improve the process for the next iteration.

MMF Selection Revisited

Once the IFM has been completed (and transitioned to the user if the element was an MMF), the process either proceeds to the next element in the sequence selected by the IFM heuristic or, if new information has come to light that changes the MMF tables (risks, projected returns, etc.), the heuristic is reapplied to the modified MMF table to generate a modified sequence (using the elements already completed as fulfilled precursors).

IFM development and delivery continues until the end of the sequence defined by the IFM heuristic or until the stakeholders determine that it no longer makes sense to develop any additional MMFs at the current time.

Summary

- This chapter describes how IFM can be implemented within the phases of the RUP lifecycle in order to provide support for financially-informed decision making. IFM elements (MMFs and AEs) are identified and specified during the early phases of inception and elaboration, and then developed iteratively during the final phases of the lifecycle.

- This approach enables the project to achieve optimal, or close to optimal, NPV (according to the characteristics of the IFM heuristic) and effectively breaks a larger project down into manageable development and delivery components.

References

1. P. Kroll and P. Kruchte. *The Rational Unified Process Made Easy: A Practitioer's Guide to the RUP,* Reading, Massachusetts: Addison Wesley, 2003.

2. P. Kruchten. *The Rational Unified Process: An Introduction,* 2nd ed. Reading, Massachusetts: Addison Wesley, 2000.

3. B. Boehm, "A Spiral Model of Software Development and Enhancement," *IEEE Computer* 21(5): 61–72, 1988.

4. B. Boehm, "Anchoring the Software Process," *IEEE Software* 13(4): 73–82, 1996.

5. The Standish Group, *Chaos Report,* 1995. Available online at http://www.standishgroup.com/visitor/chaos.htm

6. Software Engineering Institute, *Architectural Tradeoff Analysis Method,* Carnegie Mellon University. Available online at http://www.sei.cmu.edu/ata/ata_method.html

7. B. Boehm, A. Egyed, J. Kwan, D. Port, A. Shah, and R. Madachy, "Using the Win-Win Spiral Model: A Case Study," *IEEE Computer*, 31 (7): 33–44, 1998.

8. H. In and B. Boehm, "Using Win-Win Quality Requirements Management Tools: A Case Study," *Annals of Software Engineering* 11: 141–174, 2001.

IFM and Agile Development

There is a natural synergism between agile processes and the incremental funding method. Both focus on the frequent delivery of small chunks of customer-valued functionality. IFM describes a technique for ordering these chunks so as to optimize ROI.■

The Challenges

This chapter explains how to implement incremental funding practices within an agile software development project. At first glance, agile concepts may seem to conflict with IFM strategies of optimizing the delivery sequence; however, both agile development and IFM focus on the incremental delivery of customer-valued software in an environment that embraces change. This commonality of purpose supports the effective merging of these two approaches. IFM entails a deeper analysis of the benefits of each piece of functionality, requiring a closer partnership between developers and business stakeholders. Just as agile principles call for project-level decision making to be placed into the hands of the customers, IFM calls for a larger voice for the business-level stakeholders to ensure that business-level goals are considered. In today's IT environment, successful projects can only be achieved when programmers, business managers, and customers work together as a closely knit team. IFM describes how this can be accomplished.

The first part of this chapter takes an in-depth look at the application of IFM within an eXtreme programming (XP) environment. We chose XP because of its growing popularity and because its practices capture the essence of the agile movement. The second section then discusses strategies for implementing incremental funding within two other agile environments of SCRUM and feature-driven development (FDD). In this chapter we also assume a general understanding of the principles of XP. A good introduction to XP is available in Kent Beck's book *eXtreme Programming explained, Embrace Change* [1] and also online at http://www.extremeprogramming.org [2].

Perhaps one of the greatest misconceptions of the agile process is the notion that the agile developer works solely on a day-to-day basis. This misconception may have originated from the philosophy of delivering the simplest design possible for the current deliverable and not wasting time with excessive up-front design or project-level planning. In reality, one of the initial XP activities is the development of a release plan. Unlike the detailed project plan that is used to constantly track progress in traditional projects, the XP release plan provides a general outline in which the project is broken down into user stories, which are then assigned to specific releases with target release dates. The XP literature describes a release as a "small unit of functionality that makes good business sense and can be released into the customer's environment early in the project" [1,2]. Of course, change is continually embraced, and releases and their components may be adjusted in response to changing business and project needs, but this is the type of environment in which IFM thrives.

IFM brings several benefits to an agile project:

- It strengthens the current approach to requirements prioritization, providing crucial information about the costs and benefits of a particular development strategy, and enabling customers to make informed decisions.

- It provides the information needed to evaluate the impact of changing delivery strategies. This means that customers requesting a reprioritization of delivered functionality can fully understand the ROI implications of that decision.

- It provides a useful analytical tool for programmers to evaluate the costs and benefits of architectural decisions.

- Just as in a traditional project, IFM enables developers to identify a delivery sequence that optimizes ROI and, when funding is tight, to establish a development strategy that creates earlier self-funding for the project.

Incremental Development the Agile Way

Agile development is inherently an incremental approach to software development [3,2]. XP requires customers to define a set of "user stories" that describe their needs and expectations of the system. A user story, which is a brief description written by the customer describing something that the system must do, serves two primary purposes in XP. First it replaces the need for a formal requirements specification, and secondly it is used to estimate effort [2]. XP guidelines call for the system to be decomposed into approximately 60 to 100 user stories, although the exact number is obviously project dependent. Developers then estimate the duration of each user story in terms of one, two, or three weeks' worth of work. Stories smaller than one week are combined into larger ones, and those over three weeks are split into smaller ones. At a "release planning" meeting a subset of user stories are allocated to a system release. These stories then form a pool of stories that may be selected for iterations within the release. The final product at the end of the release is termed the "system release."

Each system release is physically implemented as a series of iterations. In general, an entire project might be decomposed into a dozen iterations of one to three weeks. However, larger-scale agile projects can take one or two years and 20 to 30 iterations. Prior to each iteration, the customer selects a subset of user stories from the pool of stories assigned to the release. The developers must produce a testable executable at the end of each iteration, so that the customer can start testing the product and provide early feedback. The executable may or may not have revenue-generating potential and so may or may not go into production. Iterations that go into production are often called "production-level releases."

In XP, production-level releases tend to be further apart during the early stages of a project and become more frequent as the project approaches completion. This is depicted in Figure 9.1, where we see that early production-level releases encompass three to four iterations, while later ones tend to

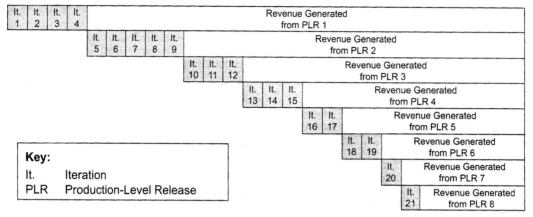

Figure 9.1
Production-Level Release Points in a Typical XP Project

occur at the end of each iteration. From an NPV perspective, it is the production-level releases that are important, because that is when delivered functionality starts to generate revenue for the customer.

Clustering User Stories into MMFs

An MMF has been defined earlier as the smallest unit of functionality that delivers clear value to the user. In some cases a user story might meet this criterion and be considered an MMF in its own right; however, in many cases it would take several user stories to produce true value-generating functionality.

Current XP practices require developers to estimate the effort needed to develop each user story. This enables them to calculate the cost of developing the story, but does not provide any quantified estimate of its benefits following delivery. Current practices simply ask the customer to select the stories that they consider most valuable, without providing clear guidelines to explain how this should be done. There is therefore no guarantee that customers will consider the business implications of their sequencing decisions.

If in fact customers do consider the perceived value of the MMF, they are likely to use the greedy approach to sequencing, in which the MMF with the highest perceived value is selected next. As demonstrated in Chapter 5, this approach does not consistently identify the delivery sequence with highest NPV.

IFM requires the additional step of evaluating and quantifying the benefits of each user story. In many cases, the customer may not be able to do this alone, and must identify relevant business stakeholders for each story and work with them to evaluate tangible and intangible benefits. Requiring a slightly more formal analysis of the value of each user story has the positive effect of making the process more inclusive, and drawing in a broader spectrum of critical stakeholders. XP has always incorporated customer and business stakeholders in the release meeting, but with IFM it becomes more important than ever to identify and involve people who can evaluate business ramifications and benefits.

In most cases, a user story must be combined with other stories to form an MMF. For example, the user story depicted in Figure 9.2 must first be combined with user stories such as "Reserve a flight," "Review reservation," and "Print flight details," before it will deliver its true value, as shown in Figure 9.3. This demonstrates that MMFs may be multigrained in an agile environment. In some cases a single user story forms an MMF, and in other cases a group of user stories form an MMF. The important factor is that an MMF must deliver specific value to the customer, definable either in terms of quantifiable ROI or as intangible benefits. Furthermore, user stories that belong within the same MMF should whenever possible be developed within a single production-level release.

It doesn't make sense to invest in developing a user story if that story is unable to return value until other, related user stories are developed in future iterations, because an underlying concept of both XP and IFM is to deliver functionality to the customer in small value-generating releases. IFM does not suggest that these stories should always be developed within a single iteration. In some cases one or two user stories from an MMF may be developed

User Story:	Time Estimate:
	3 weeks
Display Available Flights	
	Benefits Analysis:
Connect to SABRE airline reservation system and retrieve and display a list of flights that match user's preferences.	Attract new customers to the store, and reduce the workload of sales staff if the customer has already located a suitable flight.
See MMF Flight Reservation	

Figure 9.2
Benefits Analysis of a User Story

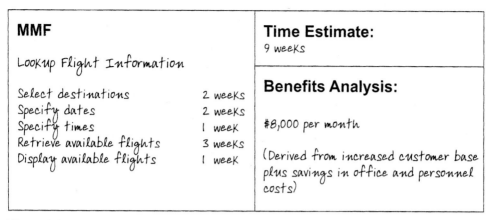

Figure 9.3
Bundling User Stories into Composite MMFs

in an earlier iteration in order to obtain early customer feedback. In terms of generating revenue, it is the production-level releases rather than the iterations that count. This is depicted in Figure 9.4, in which we see that the development of a single MMF should not straddle the boundaries of a release.

One other difference between Figures 9.4 and 9.1 involves the pacing of production-level releases. A major objective of IFM is to deliver revenue-generating functionality throughout the project. Whereas production-level releases in a typical XP project pick up steam in later stages, IFM enables earlier and more consistent delivery through deliberately creating bundles of revenue-generating user stories.

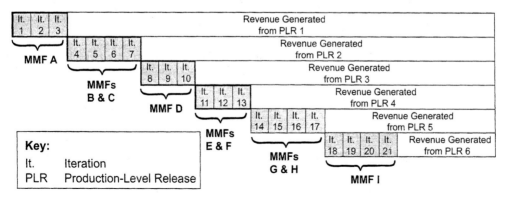

Figure 9.4
Bundling Iterations into MMFs for Production-Level Releases

All of the normal XP practices, such as distribution of user stories to developers, task breakdown, task estimations, and measurement of project velocity, occur at the user-story level. The MMF simply supports the process of analyzing and optimizing the returns on a project.

Release Planning: Bundling User Stories in Releases

Bill Wake, in his book *Extreme Programming Explored* [4], describes the XP approach to selecting user stories for iterations. Users rank the stories according to three levels of value—high, medium, and low—and the programmers similarly rank the stories according to risk—high, medium, or low. Selection then tends to be driven by delivery of high-valued user stories first, with some priority given to those with lowest risks.

One of the problems of this approach is that it does not clearly distinguish the trade-offs between long-term value to the customer and logical precedence relationships among functional units. XP clearly states that technical and architectural dependencies between components should not guide the selection strategy; however, business constraints caused by dependencies between MMFs should certainly play a major role in the delivery sequence. An MMF precedence graph visually represents these initial dependencies. To be fair, it can probably be assumed that many customers implicitly consider these factors when selecting user stories; however, without clearly emphasizing this need, there is a very real danger that stories will be delivered in an order that fails to optimize the overall value of the project.

Consider once again the online travel agency. In this example, the users might recognize the group tour organizer as a highly valued feature. The ability to organize tours online could attract significant new business and become a very large money-generating option. At the same time, this feature requires the existence of several other MMFs, including the flight reservation and local tour organizer. In the long run the ability to organize tour groups could generate significant revenue, but the logical precedence relations among user stories would likely result in this particular MMF being delivered later in the schedule, at least after the flight reservation and local tour organizer MMFs had been delivered.

The point is that the XP release plan implies a third dimension that correlates with the MMF precedence graph. In a more traditional development environment, the precedence graph captures both business and technical dependencies, but XP deliberately chooses not to allow technical considerations to dictate delivery sequences. In XP the precedence graph therefore

MMF		User Story	# of weeks
A	Look up flight information	Select destinations	2
		Specify dates	2
		Specify times	1
		Retrieve available flights	3
		Display available flights	1
B	Reserve single destination flight	Select available flight	2
		Reserve one-way flight	2
C	Reserve multi-destination flight	Reserve round-trip flight	1
D	Make payment	Online credit card payment	1
		Print receipt	0.5
E	View reservation	View itinerary	1
		View terms and conditions	1
F	Reserve seat	View multiple reservations	1
		Print receipt	0.5
		Display seat layouts	2
		Mark reserved seats	1
		Select a seat	1

Figure 9.5
User Stories for an Additional Set of MMFs

only captures business constraints defined by the customer. To illustrate this, Figure 9.5 depicts a set of user stories bundled into MMFs and composed into the precedence graph of business constraints shown in Figure 9.6.

Precedence graphs are also useful for analyzing high-risk user stories and determining whether an XP prototype, known as an architectural spike, is needed. A high-risk user story that has no MMFs dependent on it does not

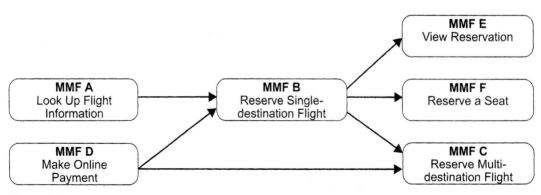

Figure 9.6
Precedence Graph Showing Business Relationships between MMFs

warrant an architectural spike until it is selected for development. In contrast, a high-risk story that sits on a critical path for other highly valued stories must be examined more closely in order to mitigate associated risks before pursuing the project.

During the release meeting, a partial precedence graph is established for any MMFs that are selected for the current release. For example, if the "reserve single destination flight" MMF and its associated user stories are selected for delivery in the first release, it should be evaluated for precedence relationships. In this case the flight reservation MMF will not generate significant value unless the MMFs for "online payment" and "look up flight information" are in place first. A decision can then be made as to whether all three MMFs can be completed during the first release. Checking for precedence relationships is an iterative process that must be executed for each MMF selected for inclusion within a release.

Assessing the NPV of the Release Plan

Once user stories have been tentatively assigned to releases, NPV and cash flow calculations can be applied to determine the value and ROI for the current plan. The process is very simple, because all user stories have previously been assigned both a duration estimate and a benefits estimate. Even though there may be close to a hundred user stories in an application, these stories are bundled into production-level releases, and cost-benefit analysis can be performed at the granularity of a release. The MMFs dictate which user stories must be delivered within the same production-level release. Lee, Guadagno, and Xiaoping refer to this as "story coupling" [5].

Figure 9.5 depicts six MMFs. All of them are composite MMFs comprised of multiple user stories, except for MMF A, which is composed of a single-story.

The SANPV for each MMF is then calculated as follows.

- **Estimate the Cost of Developing the MMF**
  The cost of developing the MMF is calculated by adding up the initial duration estimates of each story and converting the estimated effort to actual cost estimates. In effect this approach is quite similar to the traditional work breakdown structure (WBS) method, in which the work is broken down into small components, which are then estimated individually and added together to find the total cost. IFM adds the

components of each MMF, and then incorporates those results in an effort to maximize project-wide ROI.

The duration estimates can then be converted to cost through the use of a standard team multiplier based on the estimated velocity of the project team, to which additional overhead costs of the MMF are added. Project velocity is a measure of the number of user stories completed by a team during an iteration. At the start of a new project the team's velocity can only be estimated based on the velocity of similar teams working on similar projects. The velocity can be used to determine a multiplier by which duration estimates can be converted to costs. Additional costs related to extra expenses such as tool purchases are then added to the total.

- **Estimate the Benefits of the MMF**

  The benefits of each MMF are determined through market surveys, trend analysis, and predictions based on known figures. As described previously in this book, the projected revenue for each MMF should be expressed in terms of anticipated income over each subsequent period following delivery. The projected costs and revenues for our example are shown in Figure 9.7. Intangible MMFs can be evaluated using the pairwise comparison techniques described in Chapter 7.

- **Calculate Sequence-Adjusted NPV**

  An SANPV table is then constructed for these MMFs using the technique described in Chapter 3. A discount rate of 1% per period has been arbitrarily applied in this example. These results are shown in Figure 9.8 and depict the NPV for each MMF if delivered during the specified period. This table is then used during the release planning meeting to help guide the scheduling and sequencing process.

MMF	Periods											
	1	2	3	4	5	6	7	8	9	10	11	12
A	-45	8	8	8	8	8	8	8	8	8	8	8
B	-40	10	15	20	25	25	25	25	25	25	25	25
C	-5	5	5	5	5	5	5	5	5	5	5	5
D	-10	2	2	3	3	4	4	5	5	5	5	5
E	-5	5	5	5	5	5	5	5	5	5	5	5
F	-20	5	5	5	5	5	5	5	5	5	5	5

Figure 9.7
Cost and Benefits Analysis for MMFs ($US in Thousands)

MMF	Periods											
	1	2	3	4	5	6	7	8	9	10	11	12
A	38	30	23	16	8	1	-6	-13	-20	-26	-33	-40
B	188	164	140	117	94	71	48	26	4	-14	-27	-35
C	46	42	37	32	27	23	18	13	9	4	0	-4
D	30	25	21	16	11	7	3	0	-3	-5	-7	-9
E	46	42	37	32	27	23	18	13	9	4	0	-4
F	32	27	22	18	13	8	4	0	-5	-9	-13	-18

Figure 9.8
SANPV Table for MMFs at 1% / Period Discount Rate ($US in Thousands)

Release Planning Meeting

The purpose of a release planning meeting is to tentatively assign user stories to releases. This process can be successfully accomplished by using the IFM sequencing algorithms, and considering the natural breakpoints that MMFs create and at which product-level releases might naturally occur.

The team first decides on an approximate duration and project velocity for each release. For example, the team may decide that the first release should take approximately six weeks, and that they could deliver a velocity of 10 points per week. The total capacity of the release is therefore approximately 60 points. By this stage, user stories have already been evaluated and grouped into meaningful MMFs capable of delivering true value to the customer. The IFM heuristic described in Chapter 5 is then applied to identify an optimal or close-to-optimal delivery sequence. The level of concurrency within a release is driven by the capacity of the release in terms of story points, the total points needed to develop all stories within the release, and the feasibility of concurrently developing MMFs.

The IFM heuristic is then used to select MMFs and their embedded user stories for each release. In XP, this task rightly belongs to the customer, so we need to consider how the IFM heuristic serves customer's needs, and how the ordering of users stories is intrinsically driven by the customer.

By this stage, the customer has written the user stories and where necessary bundled them into MMFs. The current set of MMFs therefore reflects the customer's understanding of how user stories should be grouped in order to deliver useful and value-packed functionality. It is also the customer who identifies and quantifies the benefits of each MMF in terms of ROI. Intangibly valued MMFs have also been considered and pairwise comparisons have been made in order to determine ROI equivalence values. All of these activities represent a broad spectrum of customer-driven choices and deliberations, and provide the necessary building blocks for applying IFM sequencing strategies.

IFM sequencing identifies the most valuable MMFs for inclusion in the first release. Each MMF accepted by the customer consumes a certain number of user story points from the overall release capacity. For example, an MMF composed of three user stories with estimates of one, two, and two weeks' development time, respectively, would consume a total of five story points from the overall capacity of 60 points. The process of assigning MMFs to each release continues until the entire capacity is consumed.

The development team and customer have full discretion to order stories within the release's iterations without having significant impact on the overall ROI of the project. Any user stories that get snowplowed into the next release should, whenever possible, all be taken from the same MMF. This limits the impact of the delayed delivery to a single revenue-generating MMF.

The cost-benefit analysis obtained from this initial release plan provides a baseline against which any future release-level decisions must be made. For example, if the customer decides to bring a certain MMF forward in the release plan or to cancel another MMF entirely, IFM calculations will clearly show the impact of this decision on the project-level ROI. As stated earlier, IFM provides the tools needed for ROI-informed decision making and creates accountability at the business level.

The Architecture Question

The XP approach prescribes that architecture be "discovered" during the development process. Robert Martin [3] in his book *Agile Software Development: Principles, Patterns, and Practices,* suggests that the initial use cases of the system drive at least the early definition of the architecture. Without explicitly setting aside time for architectural design and development, XP user story estimates implicitly cover the effort of developing both functionality and architecture.

One of the most controversial issues of agile development is the XP concept of always developing the simplest possible solution needed to implement the current user story. Many people have challenged this notion, claiming that certain architectural decisions make it very difficult to rearchitect or refactor the system in the future. Agile developers are equally adamant that as long as the code is kept simple through continual refactoring, then it will always be possible to modify the system to accommodate new functionality and different architectural needs.

As we discussed in Chapter 4, IFM is architecturally neutral. In fact, although we advocate shaping candidate architectures up front, IFM architectural concepts are implicitly agile because final architectural decisions are made as needed, and architectural components are developed on a just-in-time basis. Investing months at the start of the project to build a rigid architecture sometimes can significantly reduce overall ROI through delaying the delivery of revenue-generating functionality and sometimes through building components that are never used.

Rather than debating whether the architecture must be shaped prior to the first iteration or discovered during the early iterations, we propose that decisions related to architecture should, like other decisions, be ROI-informed ones. In either case, actual development of architectural components should be delayed until they are actually needed.

In XP, architecture tends to evolve during the early iterations and is then refined during later iterations. Traditional development processes tend to deliver a more extensive architecture up front, capable of supporting much of the future functionality of the system. In contrast, XP advocates using the simplest solution necessary to support the current functionality and warns programmers against developing extensive up-front architectures. This principle is based on two primary assumptions.

The first assumption is that the simplest solution will make it possible to deliver the functionality to the customer earlier. The primary benefit is that early customer interaction with the product provides early feedback, keeping the project on target and making early revenue generation possible. The second assumption is that the customer benefits from keeping future options open, because the release plan may need to be changed for many reasons. The customer may decide to cancel planned user stories and replace them with others. The XP philosophy states that investing in future needs may prematurely and unnecessarily commit the project to a certain path, which can ultimately waste valuable resources through developing parts of the system that will never be used.

This is of course a strong argument, but one that should be evaluated in light of our ability to financially analyze the alternate options. The IFM philosophy suggests that this type of decision should be made on a case-by-case basis through considering the risks, costs, and benefits of the alternate strategies, rather than basing the decision on a blanket rule.

Simple versus Look-Ahead Solution

Consider an online document management system, in which users can access and download journal articles. They can also subscribe to online journals, request notification when new articles related to a certain topic are posted, and sign up to join topic-focused discussions.

Figure 9.9 depicts a partial view of the system showing four MMFs. Each MMF is composed of multiple user stories. Precedence relations are shown between the MMFs, indicating that MMF A, which handles basic subscriptions, must be delivered first. Following this, either MMF B or MMF C can be delivered, as neither one depends on the other from the business point of view. However, an interesting architectural trade-off exists between these two MMFs.

MMF B represents a very straightforward subscription relationship between users and journals. A customer can subscribe to one or more journals to receive its online delivery. In this case, the subscription part of the MMF could be handled quite easily with a single subscription class that interfaces with a simple subscription table.

MMF C, on the other hand, represents a more complex subscription relationship, in which customers subscribe to general topics in order to receive notification whenever a related article is posted. The notification mechanism needs the ability to rate new articles according to multiple subscription criteria and, where appropriate, to forward them to subscribers. This type of subscription requires a more robust solution, such as a publish-subscribe mechanism [6] that would allow publishers and subscribers to be

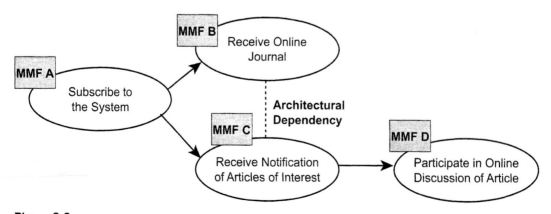

Figure 9.9
SANPVs per Period for MMFs ($US in Thousands)

added independently, and would provide a centralized event server to handle the relatively complex logic needed to support article subscriptions.

If MMF B were developed prior to MMF C, a very simple subscription infrastructure could be used, which would then need to be refactored if and when MMF C were developed. The primary advantage of this approach would be that MMF B would be less complex, and would be completed and delivered more quickly to the customer, resulting in early feedback and potential early revenue. If MMF C were delivered first, the more complex publish-subscribe architecture would be developed, which would easily accommodate the later development of MMF B.

In a traditional development environment, the architecture would be planned up front, and the publish-subscribe scheme would probably be selected. In contrast, if MMF B were selected for development first, in an agile environment, the simpler subscription scheme would be used first; then if MMF C were eventually developed it would be refactored to the publish-subscribe scheme. In both cases, decisions were based primarily on normal practices of the current development environment. But what if these decisions could be based on principles of IFM instead? What if we could analyze the costs and benefits of these decisions within the contexts of real risks and likelihoods that impacted the development of each MMF?

Consider the following, simple situation in which there are three MMFs: A, B, and C. If MMF A were developed first, we could deliver either a simple architecture or one that would also support the future development of MMF B. XP philosophy dictates the simple solution; IFM enables us to analyze this decision by calculating the impact on NPV of both approaches. Figure 9.10 depicts the costs and revenues of MMFs A, B, and C, as well as three AEs. In AE 1 a simple infrastructure is built to support D only. AE 2 captures the costs needed to refactor MMF A if MMF B is subsequently constructed. Finally, AE 3 depicts the costs of establishing the alternate and more extensible infrastructure for MMF A in the first place. To make the analysis more realistic, we

AE/MMF	Periods															
	1	2	3	4	5	6	7	8	9	10	11	12	13	14	15	16
1	-15	0	0	0	0	0	0	0	0	0	0	0	0	0	0	0
2	-10	0	0	0	0	0	0	0	0	0	0	0	0	0	0	0
3	-20	0	0	0	0	0	0	0	0	0	0	0	0	0	0	0
A	-50	10	10	10	10	10	10	10	10	10	10	10	10	10	10	10
B	-50	12	12	12	12	12	12	12	12	12	12	12	12	12	12	12
C	-10	5	5	5	5	5	5	5	5	5	5	5	5	5	5	5

Figure 9.10
Cost and Returns Analysis of MMFs and AEs ($US in Thousands)

further assume that AE 1 takes less effort to develop than AE 3, allowing MMF C and AE 1 to be developed concurrently during a single period. If MMF C is not developed in period 1, it is developed in period 2 instead.

The four options that need to be evaluated are shown in Figure 9.11 and briefly outlined below:

Option 1:   MMFs A and C, and AE 1 are all developed during period 1. MMF B is not needed.

Option 2:   MMF A and AE 3 are developed during period 1, and MMF C is developed in period 2. Because B is not developed, AE 3 represents an architectural "overkill"(i.e., wasted effort).

Option 3:   MMFs A and C and AE 1 are developed in period 1, and MMF B and AE 2 in period 2. AE2 represents the refactoring of MMF A that is needed to support MMF B.

Option 4:   MMF A and AE 3 are developed during period 1, and MMF B and C in period 2. In this case, MMF C is added without the need for refactoring because AE 3 provides its needed architectural components.

We should stress that within XP, a product-level release is composed of multiple iterations, each of which contains multiple user stories. IFM assigns stories to product-level releases, but does not attempt to sequence them within the release. The assignment of two elements to one product-level release, such as AE 1 and MMF A, therefore does not necessarily imply con-

Period	
1	2
A	
1	
C	

a. Concurrent Development Option 1

Period	
1	2
A	C
3	

b. Concurrent Development Option 2

Period	
1	2
A	B
1	2
C	

c. Concurrent Development Option 3

Period	
1	2
A	B
3	C

d. Concurrent Development Option 4

Figure 9.11
Options for Concurrent Development

current development. It is quite feasible for AE 1 to be developed in one iteration and for MMF A to be developed in a following iteration. These decisions belong entirely with the developer. In the following discussion, the term "period" is taken to mean a product-level release.

Figure 9.12 shows the NPV calculation for each of the options described on the previous page, assuming a discount rate of 0.8% per period

Initial observations show that in this example developing the simpler solution first (i.e., AE 1 as opposed to AE 3) seems like the best option. In the first case in which MMF B is ultimately never developed, we would have a

	Element	1	2	3	4	5	6	7	8	9	10	11	12	13	14	15	16	Net
Period 1	A	-50	10	10	10	10	10	10	10	10	10	10	10	10	10	10	10	100
	1	-15	0	0	0	0	0	0	0	0	0	0	0	0	0	0	0	-15
	C	-10	5	5	5	5	5	5	5	5	5	5	5	5	5	5	5	65
Cash		-75	15	15	15	15	15	15	15	15	15	15	15	15	15	15	15	150
PV @	0.80%	-74	15	15	15	14	14	14	14	14	14	14	14	14	13	13	13	135

a. Calculation of NPV for Development Option 1 ($US in Thousands)

	Element	1	2	3	4	5	6	7	8	9	10	11	12	13	14	15	16	Net
Period 1	A	-50	10	10	10	10	10	10	10	10	10	10	10	10	10	10	10	100
	3	-20	0	0	0	0	0	0	0	0	0	0	0	0	0	0	0	-20
Period 2	C		-10	5	5	5	5	5	5	5	5	5	5	5	5	5	5	60
Cash		-70	0	15	15	15	15	15	15	15	15	15	15	15	15	15	15	140
PV @	0.80%	-69	0	15	15	14	14	14	14	14	14	14	14	14	13	13	13	125

b. Calculation of NPV for Development Option 2 ($US in Thousands)

	Element	1	2	3	4	5	6	7	8	9	10	11	12	13	14	15	16	Net
Period 1	A	-50	10	10	10	10	10	10	10	10	10	10	10	10	10	10	10	100
	1	-15	0	0	0	0	0	0	0	0	0	0	0	0	0	0	0	-15
	C	-10	5	5	5	5	5	5	5	5	5	5	5	5	5	5	5	65
Period 2	B		-50	12	12	12	12	12	12	12	12	12	12	12	12	12	12	118
	2		-10	0	0	0	0	0	0	0	0	0	0	0	0	0	0	-10
Cash		-75	-45	27	27	27	27	27	27	27	27	27	27	27	27	27	27	258
PV @	0.80%	-74	-44	26	26	26	26	26	25	25	25	25	25	24	24	24	24	232

c. Calculation of NPV for Development Option 3 ($US in Thousands)

Figure 9.12
The Impact of Simple vs. Extensive Up-front Architecture on NPV

	Element	1	2	3	4	5	6	7	8	9	10	11	12	13	14	15	16	Net
Period 1	A	-50	10	10	10	10	10	10	10	10	10	10	10	10	10	10	10	100
	3	-20	0	0	0	0	0	0	0	0	0	0	0	0	0	0	0	-20
Period 2	B		-50	12	12	12	12	12	12	12	12	12	12	12	12	12	12	118
	C		-10	0	0	0	0	0	0	0	0	0	0	0	0	0	0	60
Cash		-70	-40	27	27	27	27	27	27	27	27	27	27	27	27	27	27	258
PV @	0.80%	-69	-49	26	26	26	26	26	25	25	25	25	25	24	24	24	24	232

d. Calculation of NPV for Development Option 4 ($US in Thousands)

Development Sequence	SANPV	Architecture Option	Future Actions
1	1335	Simple	MMF B is never developed
2	125	Extended	
3	232	Simple	MMF B is developed in period 2
4	232	Extended	

e. Summary of SANPVs for Each Delivery ($US in Thousands)

Figure 9.12, continued
The Impact of Simple vs. Extensive Up-front Architecture on NPV

project NPV of $135,000 if we developed the MMFs A and C and AE 1 all during the first period, and a project NPV of only $125,000 if we developed MMFs A and AE 3 in period 1 and MMF C in period 2. In this case we'd be wasting $10,000 if we developed the more complex architectural element AE 3 during period 1. The higher returns of the first option can primarily be attributed to the fact that developing the simpler solution first frees up time to develop the additional revenue generating MMF C during period 1. If MMF B were ultimately developed during period 2, and the architecture refactored through AE 2, then the resulting NPV of $232,000 is, in this case, the same as the NPV if we had initially developed the more complex architecture through the sequence of MMF A and AE 3 in period 1, followed by MMFs B and C in period 2.

The bottom line is that in this example if MMF B is never developed, we reduce costs and increase NPV of the project through taking the simpler approach. At the same time we don't lose anything if MMF B is developed in the future because the calculations show that the NPV of the refactored solution equals the NPV of the solution delivering a more extensive architecture up front! In this particular case, and many other similar examples, the XP philosophy of selecting the simplest possible solution is clearly supported. However, if the refactoring costs were greater, the analysis periods longer, or the discount rate a little higher, the IFM calculations might lead us to an entirely different conclusion. The point is that IFM enables us to make decisions on a case-by-case basis, rather than by simply following a general philosophy.

The situation is more complex when the optimal delivery sequence depends on whether a future MMF is actually developed or not. For example, consider a different situation in which taking the simpler solution would result in a loss of $10,000 if we later needed to refactor, and taking the extended solution would result in a wasted effort of $20,000 if a future MMF (that we will call MMF X) were never developed. In this situation, the best course of action could only be determined by considering the probability of developing MMF X. If there were a strong likelihood that MMF X would be developed, then it might make sense to build the more extensive architecture up front, but if there were major doubts about the future of MMF X, then it could well make sense to take the simpler approach and refactor only as needed.

To analyze this situation more formally we need to assess development and market risks, and determine the likelihood of developing MMF X in the future.

If the probability of developing MMF X is 60%, we have the following cost-adjusted risks.

- NPV risk of *not* developing the extended solution when we should have done so: $60\% \times \$10,000 = \$6,000$.

- NPV risk of developing the extended solution when the simpler solution would have sufficed: $40\% \times \$20,000 = \$8,000$.

The greater risk is therefore in the second option, and we should take the less risky first option and develop the simplest solution first.

IFM therefore brings clarity to these types of decisions. Clearly if the probabilities had been different, the proposed solution should have changed. If, for example, the likelihood of developing MMF X were 90%, then we would compare $90\% \times \$10,000 = \$9,000$ to $10\% \times \$20,000 = \$2,000$, and we would decide to develop the more extensive architecture up front.

Other Agile Development Environments

This chapter has primarily described the application of IFM principles within an XP environment. However, there are many other methods that can be used in place of XP or to complement it. This section takes a brief look at two other popular approaches to agile development. Although each of these approaches differs in what it attempts to do and in how that is accomplished, they share the theme of incremental development and delivery of customer-valued functionality. Similarly, they both benefit from IFM's ability to enable ROI-informed decision making in place of more subjective prioritization techniques.

Feature-Driven Development

Feature-driven development (FDD) is a five-stage approach to software development centered on the concept of a feature. A FDD feature is described as a "small piece of client-valued functionality that can be implemented in two weeks or less" [7]. In fact, a feature is very similar to a user story both in scope and in character. FDD introduces the additional hierarchical concepts of a feature set, described as a "grouping of business-related features," and a major feature set used as a container for grouping smaller feature sets.

For example, the major feature set "organize trip" could contain the feature sets "flight reservation" and "hotel reservation." These sets would then be decomposed into a list of features such as "enter flight preferences," "display available flights," "view flight details," "reserve flight," and "print ticket invoice." Features are initially identified through the process of developing an overall class model of the system, and in many cases a feature will correspond directly with a method in a class.

An FDD project is composed of an initial one-time start-up phase and an iterative construction phase. The start-up phase involves the three activities: developing an overall model, building a features list, and planning by feature. The construction phase is composed of two activities: design by feature and build by feature. This is illustrated in Figure 9.13.

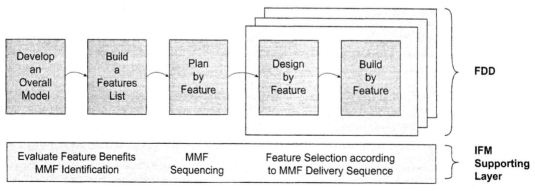

Figure 9.13
Applying IFM Principles within a Feature-Driven Development Environment

Like XP, FDD provides the building blocks needed to support an IFM process. Features deliver customer-valued functionality but are normally too small to generate income as independent units. The FDD hierarchical constructs of feature sets and major feature sets are, however, very interesting in terms of their ability to generate revenue and group features together into business units.

The primary work of identifying features occurs during the second stage of the FDD process, known as "build a features list." During this stage the team takes the model and informal features list developed in the previous stage, transforms methods into features, and identifies additional features that satisfy the customer's needs. They then group the features into feature sets and major feature sets.

Features are then prioritized as "must have," "nice to have," "add if we can," and "future." Prioritization is primarily based on the perceived or stated satisfaction of the client at having each feature implemented. As in the case of XP, prioritization fails to take into account the impact of cost-benefit analysis on the delivery schedule. Features are delivered according to the customer's need for them, even though ROI can often be optimized by ordering the delivery sequence to match business strategies instead. IFM requires the additional step of analyzing and quantifying the benefits of each feature.

Fortunately, the hierarchical groups of feature sets and major feature sets very naturally form the candidate MMFs of the system. Each feature set is tested to determine whether it can deliver either tangible revenue-generating value or other equivalent intangible benefits to the user—that is, whether is qualifies as an MMF. If a feature set does not independently meet the criterion of an MMF, it is combined with other feature sets, which are then again tested.

During the FDD plan-by-feature process, the project manager, development manager, and chief programmers determine the development sequence and set target completion dates for each feature set. At this stage the IFM heuristic can be applied to identify a delivery sequence that optimizes the value of the delivered product. An MMF precedence graph is first constructed to identify the logical business constraints placed on the delivery of the system, and then IFM processes are used to guide and inform the task of sequencing features.

The final FDD phase consists of the design-by-feature and build-by-feature processes. A chief programmer recruits feature construction team members who may work on multiple features in parallel.

According to the IFM delivery sequence plan, features must be selected from the prioritized MMFs (i.e., MMFs at the front of the delivery schedule).

Where possible, features within the same MMF should be developed in parallel. Because MMFs are the smallest units capable of delivering revenue-generating value, it would not make sense to develop 95% of an MMF but fail to deliver the 5% that transforms the MMF from a nice piece of code into a fully functioning and customer-valued unit.

Once an MMF is developed and tested, it should be released to the customer as a fully functioning piece of the completed application.

SCRUM

SCRUM is a managerial process that can be used in conjunction with other agile processes such as XP [8]. Traditional software development stages of requirements, analysis, design, evolution, and delivery are mapped to a series of fixed time intervals called "sprints." Different stages require a different number of sprints. For example, the requirements stage may take one sprint, while the evolution stage might take several sprints to complete.

SCRUM differs from other approaches in that within a sprint there is no predefined process. Instead, each sprint takes a list of work items, known as a "backlog," as its input, and outputs a series of relevant deliveries. Daily "SCRUM meetings" are held to determine which items have been completed since the last meeting, what issues or problems have been resolved, and what assignments should be completed prior to the next SCRUM meeting. These meetings are short, stand-up affairs, because SCRUM is built on the concept that process evolves on a daily basis.

Following each sprint, the product is demonstrated to the customer, partially integrated, and tested, and progress is measured through determining that the backlog has been reduced in scope.

SCRUM provides a managerial layer that can be used in conjunction with an underlying agile method such as XP. Although IFM principles are primarily implemented at the level of the underlying process, the SCRUM practices of daily meetings and end-of-sprint evaluations can effectively be used to manage and evaluate the ongoing cost-benefit analysis of a project. Several user stories or MMFs are assigned to each sprint, and each end-of-sprint evaluation provides a good opportunity for evaluating progress with respect to the initial MMF development plan and delivery sequence. Because sprints usually only last one month, they may intersect the boundaries of MMF delivery. However, to the fullest extent possible we would like to ensure that all features belonging to a single MMF are clustered within a group of consecutive sprints.

Summary

The IFM principles described in this book are equally important in both traditional and agile development environments. In each case, current practices tend to prioritize requirements either according to perceived customer satisfaction and need, or according to technical considerations. IFM adds depth to the prioritization process by requiring business and financial analysis of the benefits of each MMF. Sequencing of user stories, features, or other customer-valued functionality is then ordered to maximize a project's NPV.

- XP and IFM both deliver customer-valued functionality incrementally.

- In the XP process, user stories are combined into MMFs. Each MMF is capable of delivering either revenue-generating functionality or some comparable, intangible benefit.

- AEs required by these MMFs are identified and implemented in the agile approach; however, IFM provides visibility into the financial impact of different options.

- All stories belonging to a single MMF should be delivered during a single release, although stories can be freely allocated to any iteration within that release.

- IFM cost-benefit analysis is applied to the XP release plan to identify the optimal allocation of MMFs to releases.

- IFM analysis enables agile developers to make ROI-informed architectural decisions that consider the costs and risks involved in alternate solutions.

References

1. Kent Beck, *Extreme Programming Explained: Embrace Change,* Reading, Massachusetts: Addison Wesley, 1999.

2. Don Wells, "eXtreme Programming: A Gentle Introduction," January 26, 2003. Available online at http://www.extremeprogramming.org

3. Robert Martin, *Agile Software Development: Principles, Patterns, and Practices,* Upper Saddle River, New Jersey: Prentice Hall, 2003.

4. Bill Wake, *Extreme Programming Explored,* Boston, Massachussetts: Addison Wesley, 2001.

5. C. Lee, L. Guadagno, and J. Xiaoping, "FLUID: Requirements Authoring and Traceability," Proceedings of the Midwest Software Engineering Conference, Chicago, Illinois, 2003. Available online at: http://se.cs.depaul.edu/ise/msec2003

6. S. Gupta, J. Hartkopf, and S. Ramaswamy, "Event Notifier: A Pattern of Event Notification," *Java Report* 3(7): 1998. Also available online at http://www.users. qwest.net/~hartkopf/notifier

7. Stephen Palmer and John Felsing, *Practical Guide to Feature-Driven Development*, Upper Saddle River, New Jersey: Prentice Hall, 2002.

8. Mike Beedle, Ken Schwaber, and Robert C. Martin, *Agile Software Development with SCRUM*, Upper Saddle River, New Jersey: Prentice Hall, 2001.

Informed Decision Making

There are many factors besides NPV that affect the success of a project. Issues such as the initial investment requirement and the time needed to reach self-funding or breakeven status may also play a significant role in determining whether a project is funded. This chapter discusses trade-offs and techniques for reducing the initial cash investment needed to get a project started and for reducing the time it takes to reach self-funding. Applying these techniques can change the funding requirements of a project, making it more attractive to financial backers and ultimately increasing the odds of getting the project funded.■

A Collaborative Approach

IFM takes a financially responsible approach to developing software systems. As such, it requires a new and closer synergism between developers and business stakeholders. Although many developers are adept at estimating the cost and effort a project will require, they may be hard pressed to understand the intricacies of market trends and the business implications of a software product in sufficient detail to define its projected revenues. Business stakeholders, on the other hand, have a much better understanding of the marketplace, but while they are better able to project revenues for a software project, they have little understanding of the role of the development process itself in maximizing that value.

Unfortunately, the IT industry often does not see and manage software development as an ROI value-generating activity. Developers prefer to talk in terms of value generation without developing related revenue projections. Business stakeholders usually don't realize that delivery sequences and architectural options can have a significant impact on project-level ROI.

Clearly, software development requires a more financially responsible approach, not only at the managerial level but also at the development level where day-to-day decisions are being made by programmers and architects.

The situation clearly calls for a close collaboration between developers and business stakeholders, in which both groups contribute their expertise to the project. Many development processes already recognize that the customer's role in the selection and ordering of requirements is critical. IFM simply adds financial rigor to the process.

IFM does not prescribe an ROI-driven approach, in which all strategies and decisions must give way to the absolute authority of hard cash projections. Rather, it values the customer's interests and concerns, whether or not they translate into optimal cash returns. Many organizations are no longer willing to invest in nebulous, high-risk development projects. Instead they demand that each software investment should return clear benefits over a fairly short period of time.

Instead of dictating a strict project plan, IFM proposes a delivery schedule that optimizes the NPV of the overall project. If customers, developers, or even managers choose to override this suggestion, they do so knowing how their decision might affect the projected ROI. In fact, IFM encourages what-if queries that balance different aspects of the project in an ROI-informed manner.

IFM provides many useful pieces of information about a project. It identifies the maximum anticipated returns based on the inclusion of tangible and intangible features. It also clearly identifies the bottom line returns of the project by excluding intangible returns, as well as the lost opportunity costs associated with including intangible MMFs, with their potentially riskier return options, in the delivery sequence.

Furthermore, as we discuss later in this chapter, IFM also suggests strategies for changing critical, project-level characteristics, such as the amount of cash needed during the initial investment period, the net present value of the project, the time needed to reach self-funding status, and the time until the project breaks even in discounted cash flow terms. As we shall see later, there is often a trade-off between these factors and their related objectives.

Getting a Project Funded

Getting a project funded is one of its first major hurdles. Business-level authorization is generally only available when there is a clear financial justification. The well-documented case of the Californian Department of Motor Vehicles (DMV) software debacle, discussed in Chapter 8, clearly illustrates the importance of this point [1]. IFM strategies would have incrementally delivered useful parts of the system and would not have permitted the project to proceed without clearly measured and quantified value.

Figure 10.1 is a reprise of a figure already introduced in Chapter 2, and depicts several critical phases and event points in a project. An initial investment period at the start of the project funds initial expenses and development costs. The self-funding point of a project occurs once the revenue from delivered MMFs is sufficient to cover future development costs. At this point the project enters a new phase, known as the payback period. During this period, revenue funds ongoing development efforts and repays the initial investment. The project reaches breakeven status when the initial investment is paid off (in discounted cash flow terms). At that time, the project enters the profit period.

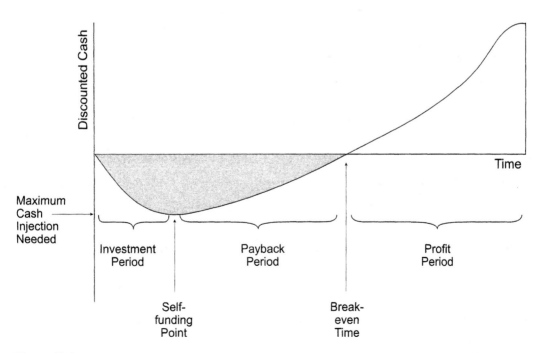

Figure 10.1
Key Points in the Discounted Cash Flow of an Application Development Project

Of course this graph oversimplifies the situation, because cash flow graphs don't necessarily follow the idealized curve depicted in the Figure. However, it does serve to identify critical events and phases that occur in the project's cash flow.

One other interesting factor highlighted in Figure 10.1 is the "maximum indebtedness" that occurs, usually sometime shortly after the start of the project. This represents the investment in the project. From a managerial point of view, we may be interested in balancing a number of factors, such as the total NPV versus the initial investment requirement, or the initial investment requirement versus the time needed to reach breakeven status.

Consider the two graphs shown in Figure 10.2. In both cases the NPV of the project is the same; however, in case (a) a smaller investment is required to sustain the project than in case (b). Even though both projects successfully repay the investment, the second project may be favored because of its lower investment cost. Most organizations have a limited amount of money available for investing in development, so a smaller investment up front might mean that an additional project could be concurrently supported. In other cases, an organization may simply not have the funds to support a project requiring a large up-front investment.

To understand the financial dynamics of a project, we need to be able to calculate all of these critical factors.

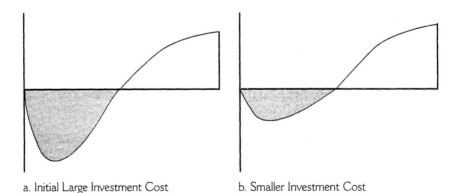

a. Initial Large Investment Cost   b. Smaller Investment Cost

Figure 10.2
Different Cash Flow Possibilities

Manipulating Project Characteristics

IFM provides the means for analyzing an existing delivery sequence and manipulating its critical features. As we pointed out earlier, the delivery sequence that returns the greatest NPV is often not the one that results in the earliest self-funding point or the one that requires the smallest investment. The IFM heuristic attempts to maximize the NPV of the project. Managers can then take that sequence, analyze its performance with respect to other critical project characteristics, and if necessary make critical trade-off decisions.

For example, although the potential NPV of a project might look very promising, the project may not be fundable because the initial investment is deemed too large and will take too long to be repaid. Managers or project sponsors might decide that they would, for example, be willing to approve the project if the self-funding point could be brought forward by two periods while maintaining the NPV at 95% of its current levels.

It might be possible to do this by moving certain MMFs forward in the delivery sequence. These MMFs must be able to generate significant revenue as soon as they are developed, in order to fund development of remaining MMFs sooner. In other words, we are interested in MMFs that are able to hit the ground running and not those that may require a longer ramp-up period.

A slight variation of the IFM heuristic enables us to identify these MMFs. Normally the IFM heuristic analyzes the sequence-adjusted NPV of each strand over the remaining analysis period. If we want to find an early self-funding point, we might be more interested in identifying strands that return high NPV within two or three periods rather than over all the remaining periods. We can adjust the IFM heuristic to do just this.

Consider the three MMFs shown in Figure 10.3 and their related period 1 NPVs, shown in Figure 10.4, assuming a discount rate of 0.8% per period. Clearly, MMF C returns the greatest NPV, $555,000, if it is delivered in period 1 and analyzed over 16 periods. However, the same MMF analyzed over 12 and 8 periods returns $201,000 and $24,000, respectively. Clearly this

MMF	Cost / Revenue per Period															
	1	2	3	4	5	6	7	8	9	10	11	12	13	14	15	16
A	-100	35	35	35	35	35	35	35	35	35	35	35	35	35	35	35
B	-100	31	32	33	34	35	36	37	38	39	40	42	43	44	46	47
C	-100	10	12	14	17	21	25	30	36	43	52	62	74	89	107	128

Figure 10.3
MMFs Used for Breakeven Point Analysis ($US in Thousands)

MMF	Number of Analysis Periods			
	16	12	8	4
A	390	265	136	3
B	436	276	129	-5
C	555	201	24	-64

Figure 10.4
NPV Analysis over a Reduced Analysis Period ($US in Thousands)

MMF requires a fairly long time before delivering its promised returns. In contrast, MMF A, which looked less interesting when evaluated over the entire analysis period, returns a much higher NPV over 8 periods than MMF C. Bringing MMF A forward in the delivery sequence would therefore bring the self-funding point forward. Unfortunately, that would also negatively affect the NPV.

Projects that require early self-funding should therefore apply the IFM algorithm in the context of reduced-period SANPV analysis, in order to identify MMFs with significant early returns that can affect project-level self-funding and breakeven times. Even though we may use a reduced-period analysis to support the sequencing process, we must use a full-period analysis to calculate the NPV of the project.

Obviously, determining how many periods to consider in the reduced analysis is a crucial decision. If the analysis duration is too short, none of the MMFs will have a chance to generate revenue. Similarly, if the analysis duration is too long, changes in sequencing may not be significant enough to affect self-funding and breakeven characteristics. This is a project-level decision that should be made after observing the typical breakeven points of individual MMFs. Alternately, because the IFM sequencing algorithm is very simple to implement, a staggered approach can be taken, using progressively shorter analysis durations until an acceptable balance of breakeven point and project-level ROI is reached.

We should temper this discussion by observing that some projects will never deliver the returns demanded by the business or may never be able to fulfill self-funding or breakeven requirements. IFM can only manipulate these factors within the constraints of the individual project. No matter how cleverly we may try to reorder MMFs, certain projects may require longer investment periods than the stakeholders are willing to support, and the ideal of self-funding may be little more than a pipe dream. Nonetheless, IFM enables us to understand the particular characteristics of the project and to make sometimes difficult decisions about whether a project can and should proceed.

The IFM Window

Another useful concept, applicable to extremely large and complex endeavors as well as to agile development projects, is the IFM window. In his book *Principles of Software Engineering Management* Tom Gilb refers to the IBM Federal Systems Division 200 person-year LAMPS project, delivered successfully over four years in 45 incremental deliveries [2].

For extremely large projects like this, MMFs may need to be prioritized into a major release plan, in which high-priority MMFs are selected for consideration in the current sequencing plan and other MMFs are deferred. An IFM window identifies which MMFs are available for sequencing. At the start of each MMF iteration, the sequencing plan is revisited, and if the priority of an MMF has changed the MMF could be moved either into or out of the active project window. Figure 10.5a depicts a current view of the project, while Figure 10.5b depicts a future view in which certain MMFs have been completed, others are currently available for sequencing, and still others have been given low priority and are deferred for future consideration.

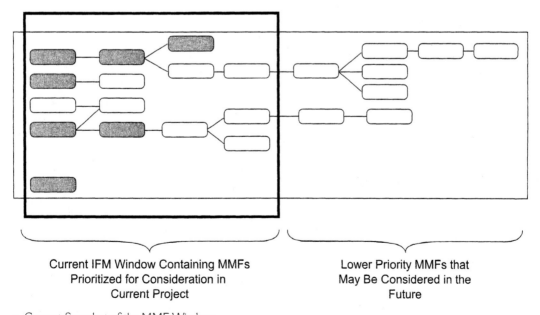

| Current IFM Window Containing MMFs Prioritized for Consideration in Current Project | Lower Priority MMFs that May Be Considered in the Future |

a. Current Snapshot of the MMF Window

Figure 10.5
An IFM Window Provides a View of Currently Sequenceable MMFs

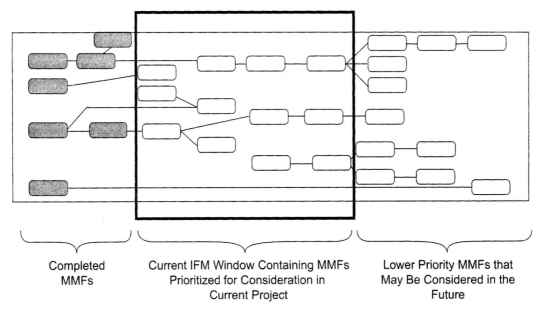

| Completed MMFs | Current IFM Window Containing MMFs Prioritized for Consideration in Current Project | Lower Priority MMFs that May Be Considered in the Future |

b. Future Snapshot of the MMF Window

Figure 10.5, continued
An IFM Window Provides a View of Currently Sequenceable MMFs

Implementing IFM Processes

Introducing new techniques into an organization can be quite a challenge [3,4]. In fact, many process improvement efforts have failed because they have been introduced in a haphazard fashion. Any organization must carefully evaluate the effort introducing a new process will require against the benefits that effort will return.

IFM is no different. However, IFM can be applied quite simply in most iterative software development environments and so does not require excessive training or start-up costs. We should therefore ask ourselves not how difficult it will be to implement IFM in our organizations, but how we could afford *not* to introduce financially responsible development strategies.

The benefits are clear. IFM not only provides a basis for project-level decision making, but it also provides the means of changing the project characteristics in order to make a project more fundable. In today's challenging IT environment, this financially responsible approach to software development just makes sense.

The Impact of IFM Strategies on Commercial Frameworks

Increasingly businesses are being urged to focus on their core competencies. When a business does not perceive IT to be a core competency, the option to outsource application development, or even the day-to-day management and support of its software applications, becomes attractive. Systems integrators who have created a core competency in application development or software consultancy become valuable partners in such cases. Negotiating contracts on these partnerships is critical to the success of the endeavor. This section examines current practices related to software development contracts and explains why the IFM incremental approach to development and delivery provides a suitable framework for such contracts.

Although contract principles have characterized the market for outsourced application development for some time, the nature of outsourcing contracts varies greatly. One of the areas of greatest variability is in the area of payment.

When an application development house writes software for a customer, staged payments by the customer are usually considered desirable. However, the metrics against which they are made can become an area of great debate and disagreement. In a traditional, monolithic software development model, the customer may reasonably withhold payment until the application has been completed. However, few if any systems integrators will accept this arrangement. The financial risk is too great, the effect this has on cash flow is too severe, and the potential for disagreement over completion criteria is always a possibility.

Staged payments benefit both the systems integrator and the customer because the reduced financial exposure allows the integrator to reduce contingencies in the pricing. In addition, because the application has been broken into manageable chunks, acceptance becomes a rolling event. Pieces of the functionality are handed over to the customer and paid for early and corrections that are required as a result of misunderstandings can be made mid-course rather than as expensive, after-the-fact, reengineering exercises.

The Achilles heel of this approach is that more often than not the client partitions and orders the application functionality rather arbitrarily. Often the granularity is insufficient or the MMFs are not sequenced correctly to provide a reasonable cash flow to the systems integrator. Furthermore, the acceptance criteria are defined in terms that may be meaningful to the client, but often vague or open to reinterpretation by the integrator. Sometimes stage payments are made against metrics that are unrelated to functionality, such as lines of code or hours of consultancy time, which certainly introduce the potential for manipulation.

It is not enough for stage payments to be defined against features that relate to the business drivers of the project. They must also be mapped to terms that are meaningful to the integrator and directly related to project progress and success metrics. This supports synchronization of the integrator's activities to the client's business and provides the client with genuine visibility into the application development progress.

IFM is the key to solving this problem. We established as early as Chapter 3 that MMFs provide a powerful vehicle for synchronizing vocabulary between client and integrator. The completion and delivery of an MMF also provides a natural point at which to schedule stage payments. The integrator has already planned the development schedule around these units, and the client clearly receives direct financial value from their delivery. Because both parties agree to their definition at the outset, the basis for payment doesn't appear to be arbitrarily defined by the client or the integrator. MMF-based stage payments also make the client's financial planning more straightforward, because the activities of the integrator can be closely correlated with the revenue stream of the business.

In fact, if the integrator not only develops the application but also supports it on behalf of the client, then IFM introduces the possibility for an even closer synchronization with the client's revenue stream. In this case, IFM enables a pay-per-use arrangement that offers the client and the integrator a high degree of control and confidence [5].

Because the integrator has visibility into the returns expected from each MMF, and assuming that the contractual framework provides the integrator, with the flexibility to sequence MMFs for maximum returns, then the opportunity exists to optimize the development.

This is particularly relevant if the integrator is replaced by an application service provider (ASP), or if the integrator acts as an ASP. In effect, the breakeven point becomes the ASP's point of profitability and the self-funding point represents the end of the investment period by the ASP or client. IFM can predict this by getting the client and the client's business partners to be as accurate as possible in the revenue predictions, giving the ASP unique financial advantages when IFM principles are applied. Contingency can be reduced, resulting in more competitive pricing, and business costs can be more accurately predicted. From the ASP perspective, this exposes the revenue and costs of the granular application to the detailed financial models described in this book.

IFM and the ASP model are therefore closely aligned. Indeed, where the ASP model uses pay-per-use or pay-per-transaction pricing, IFM uniquely empowers ASPs to optimize and provide valuable feedback to the client's business by facilitating dialog about the returns of specific MMFs and how these returns may be altered or achieved. In a 100% outsourced environment, even the pricing itself may be a matter for the ASP, in which case IFM has empowered the ASP with a combined financial and technical perspective on the application that allows it to plan and predict its revenue stream.

How Management Benefits from IFM

Management clearly benefits when IFM is applied in a project because it provides visibility into the financial and technical progress of the project. Typically, project managers use technical metrics to measure the progress of a project or the impact of unexpected events. In IFM, these metrics are also financial because the unit of sequencing is fundamentally a financial one—the MMF.

Thus project-planning or scheduling decisions translate immediately to investment changes and revenue projection modifications, without placing the burden on the project manager to perform this translation for a management audience.

When Projects Go Wrong

Probably one of the most important contributions of IFM is its provision for managing the project when things don't go as expected. For all the predictions and estimates of costs, risks, and revenues, projects are constantly impacted by changes in the environment and specific development problems that may not have been accurately predicted. Our best-laid plans may not always turn out the way we had anticipated.

For this reason, IFM is deliberately designed to be both proactive and reactive. Delivery sequences can be reevaluated prior to the start of every MMF iteration. Changes in the marketplace or the project team may affect previous decisions and cause a change of direction. An MMF that turned out to be more difficult to develop than previously anticipated could also cause project-level priorities and strategies to be reconsidered.

Consider the cash-flow diagram in Figure 10.6. In the projected cash flow represented by (a), the projected costs and revenues paint a reasonably rosy picture of the project. Unfortunately, the actual cash flow, shown as the solid line (labeled b), fails to live up to expectations. By the point in time labeled "Strategic Decision Point" on the graph, it is apparent that the project is slipping into debt. If left unmanaged it might well deliver the extremely gloomy cash flow labeled as the "death march" [6] in line c.

IFM strategies provide the means to manage this type of problem. If necessary, an individual MMF can be abandoned or rescheduled, without affecting the remainder of the project. Although this may seem like a waste of expended resources, this type of courageous decision may be exactly what is needed to save millions of dollars in future costs on what may well be a doomed project [6]. When this occurs, the problem MMF can be replaced with other more promising MMFs, with the primary objective of changing the momentum of the cash flow and regaining some of the potential revenue of the project. This scenario is labeled (b) in the diagram.

We shouldn't underestimate the value provided by IFM's ability to make this type of midcourse correction. Well-documented accounts abound of IT projects that were abandoned after millions of dollars of costs and with zero

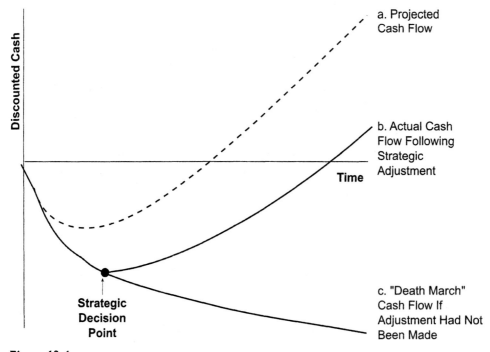

Figure 10.6
Controlling a Project through IFM Informed Corrective Actions

returns. The IFM allowance for midcourse analysis and redirection can help stave off this sort of disaster by providing us with a financially rigorous analysis of options when midcourse corrections are needed.

Where Next?

Once equipped with an understanding of the principles and practices of IFM, the next step is to put it into practice. You can use an interactive and downloadable tool available on the IFM Web site to input cost and revenue projections for your next project, and to apply IFM heuristics to identify a potential delivery sequence. We encourage you to download this tool and put IFM principles to use for your next software development project.

Chapter 11 describes a case study in which IFM is applied to the development of a Web-facing banking portal. This case study incorporates many of the principles and practices described in this book, and provides a realistic example of IFM in action.

Summary

This chapter discusses some of the critical trade-offs that may occur in the real world in order to make a project more attractive to its potential financial backers. The financial success of a project is a result of close collaboration between developers and business stakeholders. IFM provides the following critical support structures to these stakeholders throughout the project:

- IFM provides a collaboration framework in which the expertise of both the development organization and the business can be applied to optimize the value of a software project.

- IFM not only enables the optimization of NPV, but also provides the data needed to make informed trade-offs between a number of project-level factors related to self-funding status, breakeven times, and investment requirements.

- IFM provides a framework to support financially attractive stage payment contracts.

- IFM introduces the possibility of a financially rigorous analysis of pay-by-use options.

References

1. The Standish Group, *Chaos Report*, 1995. Available online at: http://www.standishgroup.com/visitor/chaos.htm

2. Tom Gilb, *Principles of Software Engineering Management*, Reading, Massachusetts: Addison Wesley, 1988.

3. P. Kroll and P. Kruchten, *The Rational Unified Process Made Easy: A Practioner's Guide to the RUP*, Boston, Massachusetts: Addison Wesley, April 2003.

4. R. Grady, *Successful Software Process Improvement*, Upper Saddle River, New Jersey: Prentice Hall, June 1997.

5. L. Ferreira, R. Dahab, M. Poggi Aragao, J. Magalhaes, "Two Approaches for Pay-per-User Software Construction," *IEEE Workshop on Advanced Issues of E-Commerce and Web/based Information Systems*, June, 2002, California, pp. 184–191.

6. E. Yourdon, *Death March*, Upper Saddle River, New Jersey: Prentice Hall, 1999.

A Case Study: IFM in Action

We now demonstrate the IFM principles in an example project, comparing the IFM heuristic and the greedy heuristic, and evaluating their results against all possible sequences. ▣

Introduction

In this chapter we illustrate the IFM principles using a hypothetical project—construction of a financial services portal for a retail bank—designed to demonstrate the methodology in action.

The bank wants to develop a Web-facing application to provide its customers with a range of transactional and informational services. The development costs are to be offset by a mixture of new account revenue and operational savings from the business.

As is the case in many portal projects, there are distinctly identifiable parts of the functionality matrix, each with its own development durations and returns. In this example, there are six MMFs. However, it is far from clear how the construction should proceed in order to provide maximum or even satisfactory returns. We need to determine which features should be developed first, which architectural elements should be constructed, when they should be constructed, how the differing risks for each feature play into the model, and what the project return is likely to be, given these variables. IFM brings clarity to these ambiguities.

So far as the financial context is concerned, the bank requires that the project produce a positive ROI after four years. Development work is constrained to take place in the first two years. Financial analysis will be performed quarterly.

In this case study we follow IFM through the process of defining MMFs, collecting and computing the financials associated with those MMFs, and applying the heuristics to determine sequence selection.

Several important simplifications have been applied in this case study in order to enhance readability and understanding. These will be pointed out as we go, together with comments on how things would be different if these simplifications were not present. To improve clarity, values in spreadsheets have generally been rounded to the nearest whole number, except where greater detail is needed.

IFM Element Definition Phase

Selecting MMFs

Following detailed consultation with the customer's marketing organization, and using IFM principles as outlined in Chapter 3, we have defined the MMFs shown in Figure 11.1.

To add concept and background to the example, a brief description of each MMF is provided below. These MMFs are examples only and are of necessity simplified in their descriptions. Nevertheless they illustrate the basic IFM concepts.

MMF	Feature
A	Display current balance
B	Display last 10 transactions
C	Display current or prior statement in electronic form
D	Transfer funds
E	Manage bill payees and pay bills
F	Apply for credit card

Figure 11.1
MMF Descriptions

MMF A: Display Current Balance   This feature allows a customer to display the current balance of his or her bank account(s).

MMF B: Display Last 10 Transactions   This feature offers a simplified display of the past 10 transactions on a customer's account(s), sufficient to support a displayed balance but without the detail of a full statement.

MMF C: Display Statement   This feature displays a customer's current or past statements in electronic form.

MMF D: Transfer Funds   This feature allows a customer to initiate domestic or international funds transfer from his or her account.

MMF E: Manage Bill Payees and Pay Bills   These features provide facilities for the management of bill payees. Because they do not represent a marketable feature, these facilities alone do not meet the requirements of an MMF. However, when merged with facilities to initiate bill payment, this aggregation of functionality can now be represented as an MMF.

MMF F: Apply for Credit Card   This feature permits a customer to apply electronically for a credit card. It does not provide any transactional capability (other than form submission) but it is readily identifiable as an MMF through the cost savings from avoiding manual forms processing.

Defining MMF Strands

The facilities in MMFs A, B, and C have a dependency relationship. The facilities in B build on those delivered in A. Similarly, the facilities in C build on those delivered in B. These three MMFs are therefore interdependent and form an MMF strand.

Likewise, the facilities of MMF E build on those delivered in D, meaning that E and D also constitute an MMF strand.

MMF F can be developed independently of any of the others. It is therefore its own strand.

Figure 11.2 summarizes this situation.

Eliciting Architectural Elements

A high-level architectural review suggests a connectivity framework for the system, as depicted in Figure 11.3.

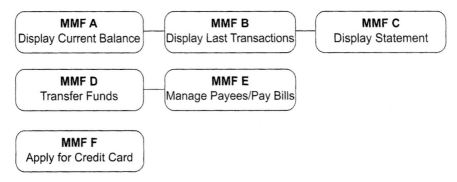

Figure 11.2
MMF Strands

Architectural elements include a simple messaging system, a transaction monitor, forms processing, Web server infrastructure, an application server, an authentication server, and a load balancer. These are listed in Figure 11.4.

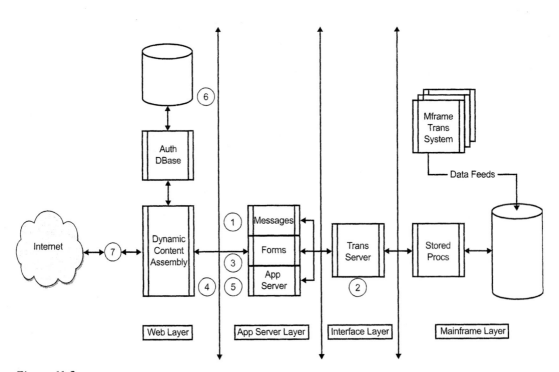

Figure 11.3
High-level Connectivity Architecture

Ref	Architectural Element (AE)	Description
1	Simple messaging	Informational interface to bank's systems of record
2	Transaction monitor	Transactional interface to bank's system of record
3	Forms processing	Processing and routing of application forms
4	Web server infrastructure	Facilitate Web-facing applications
5	Application server	Container for business objects
6	Authentication system	Controls access
7	Load balancer	Control/routes sessions

Figure 11.4
Table of Architectural Elements

The bank has decided it will outsource the hosting of the system to an ASP. The ASP provides architectural elements 4 through 7 as part of its service agreements. This leaves the bank with the responsibility of constructing or purchasing only elements 1 through 3.

Defining Architectural Dependencies

The six MMFs depend on architectural elements 1 through 3, as shown in Figure 11.5. MMFs A, B, and C depend on the messaging system. MMFs D and E depend on the transaction monitor. MMF F depends on the forms processing and routing.

Construct IFM Precedence Graph

Merging the information relating to MMFs, AEs, and their dependencies results in the precedence graph shown in Figure 11.6. The same information can also be represented using the table of precursors depicted in Figure 11.7.

Description	MMF	AE	Description
Display balance	A	1	Messaging
Display last 10 transactions	B	1	Messaging
Display statement	C	1	Messaging
Funds transfer	D	2	Transaction monitor
Manage payees, pay bills	E	2	Transaction monitor
Apply for credit card	F	3	Forms processing /routing

Figure 11.5
Architectural Dependencies

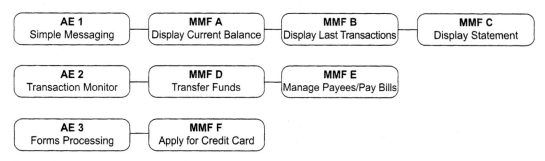

Figure 11.6
IFM Precedence Graph

IFM Element	Precursor
1	
A	1
B	A
C	B
2	
D	2
E	D
3	
F	3

Figure 11.7
Precursors Table

Financial Phase

Once the MMFs have been defined and their dependencies identified, the next step involves constructing the MMF costs-and-returns table. Analysis of the MMFs and AEs reveals the following information.

MMF A: Display Current Balance

This feature is expected to return relatively moderate cost savings of $90,000 per quarter initially, mostly through reductions in call-center time. The returns are expected to ramp down as the market becomes more demanding and because most customers want to see account balances in context. MMF A will ultimately be replaced by MMFs B and C. The estimated development time for MMF A is just one quarterly period.

MMF B: Display Last 10 Transactions

MMF B delivers savings starting at $90,000 per quarter and ramping up to $225,000 per quarter. It takes two quarterly periods to construct.

MMF C: Display Statement

MMF C provides significant savings in the form of reduced printing and mailing costs as well as additional revenue from the acquisition of new customers attracted by electronically delivered statements. Electronic statement production and delivery is complex and requires two quarters to develop. Once complete, it initially returns savings of $80,000 per quarter, which quickly ramps up to $320,000 as the customer base increases and users become more familiar with electronic statements.

MMF D: Transfer Funds

MMF D is a little trickier and more costly to develop than MMFs A and B. It results in returns that range from $45,000 per quarter to $180,000 per quarter as the market increases, mostly as a result of avoiding the costs of manual processing. The construction time is two quarterly periods.

MMF E: Manage Bill Payees and Pay Bills

The development cost for MMF E is considerable, but the returns are significant, due primarily to reduced check-processing costs and the acquisition of new customers looking for electronic bill-payment facilities. This feature returns $35,000 per quarter initially, ramping up to $245,000 per quarter as a result of advertising, customer incentives, and the increasing number of merchants and payees preconfigured in the directory.

MMF F: Apply for Credit Card

Electronic application for a credit card is a lightweight development effort (mostly a Web form and some integration with back-end systems to check account records and credit reference databases). The return is similarly lightweight and is primarily achieved through reduced application processing costs. It delivers $90,000 per quarter initially, and $135,000 per quarter thereafter. It takes two quarterly periods to construct.

AE 1: Messaging

AE 1 is relatively straightforward, incurring a total purchase, installation, and capitalized support cost of $200,000. The installation and integration time is estimated at one quarterly period.

AE 2: Transaction Monitor

This important AE provides the transactional interface to the bank's records (there are many). It's a more expensive element than AE 1, costing $400,000 to purchase and integrate. The estimated installation and integration time is one quarterly period.

MMF	Period															
/ AE	1	2	3	4	5	6	7	8	9	10	11	12	13	14	15	16
1	-200	0	0	0	0	0	0	0	0	0	0	0	0	0	0	0
A	-200	90	90	81	72	63	54	45	36	27	18	9	0	0	0	0
B	-200	-200	90	117	144	171	198	225	225	225	225	225	225	225	225	225
C	-200	-200	80	112	144	176	208	240	272	304	320	320	320	320	320	320
2	-400	0	0	0	0	0	0	0	0	0	0	0	0	0	0	0
D	-250	-250	45	72	90	108	126	144	162	180	180	180	180	180	180	180
E	-350	-350	35	70	105	140	175	210	245	245	245	245	245	245	245	245
3	-200	0	0	0	0	0	0	0	0	0	0	0	0	0	0	0
F	-100	-100	90	90	135	135	135	135	135	135	135	135	135	135	135	135

Figure 11.8
Costs and Returns of the IFM Elements (MMFs and AEs)

AE 3: Forms Processing and Routing

This third-party form router and handler created to support the credit card application facility is expected to cost $200,000 and take one quarterly period to install, test, and integrate.

Figure 11.8 summarizes the costs and returns of the various IFM elements.

Computation Phase

We now have all the data necessary to compute the metrics and derived values essential for the IFM heuristic. The first step involves calculating the SANPVs. These represent the NPV for an MMF or strand of MMFs if developed during a specified period.

Sequence-Adjusted NPVs

The IFM heuristic examines the development strands and compares their relative costs and returns at each period throughout the lifecycle of the project in order to predict the optimal sequence.

A strand is any single IFM element, any branch of the precedence graph, and, for the reasons explained in Chapter 5, any subset thereof. In other words, it is any valid combination of IFM elements in sequence, however short or long. Although certain strands may not be available for development in early periods, we find it simpler to calculate the entire table up front.

An examination of the precursors table reveals that there are a total of 19 strands in this project. Nine of these are simply the MMFs and AEs in stand-alone form. The remaining entries are the combination strands. We have applied the convention introduced in Chapter 5 and represent multiperiod elements through the use of a period (.). Thus, MMF B is represented in the table as "**B.**" indicating that it requires a second period to complete its development.

To proceed with IFM sequencing, we need to know the NPV of each strand for each potential development period—the SANPVs. The SANPVs identify promising delivery sequences and, equally importantly, help determine whether a strand is worth starting during a particular period. For example, given the constraint by the bank that this Web portal must return a profit by end of the analysis period, we can examine the SANPV table to determine the latest feasible development period for which this objective can be met for a given strand.

In our example we've assumed that the bank makes internal funds available to support the project at an advantageous rate of between 4% and 5% a year. A discount rate of 1% per quarterly period has therefore been used. Applying this discount rate and using the NPV computation methods set out in Chapter 2, we get the SANPVs shown in Figure 11.9. This table reveals several interesting pieces of information about the project, even at this early stage.

Strand	Period															
	1	2	3	4	5	6	7	8	9	10	11	12	13	14	15	16
1	-198	-196	-194	-192	-190	-188	-187	-185	-183	-181	-179	-177	-176	-174	-172	-171
2	-396	-392	-388	-384	-381	-377	-373	-369	-366	-362	-359	-355	-351	-348	-345	-341
3	-198	-196	-194	-192	-190	-188	-187	-185	-183	-181	-179	-177	-176	-174	-172	-171
A	357	353	350	346	343	332	313	287	254	214	166	111	49	-20	-96	-171
1A	155	154	152	151	141	125	101	69	31	-15	-68	-128	-195	-270	-343	-171
B.	2086	1876	1667	1460	1256	1054	853	655	458	264	94	-51	-172	-270	-343	-171
C.	2712	2415	2121	1830	1542	1256	974	707	471	263	85	-64	-185	-278	-343	-171
D.	1314	1149	985	824	663	505	348	192	54	-68	-174	-264	-337	-394	-429	-213
E.	1732	1508	1286	1066	849	634	420	209	1	-177	-323	-438	-522	-576	-600	-298
F.	1437	1309	1182	1056	932	808	686	566	446	328	210	94	-21	-96	-171	-85
2D.	753	593	435	279	124	-29	-181	-316	-434	-536	-622	-692	-746	-777	-558	-341
3F.	1111	986	862	739	618	498	379	261	145	29	-85	-198	-272	-345	-258	-171
AB.	2232	2020	1810	1602	1396	1185	968	746	518	308	115	-61	-220	-363	-266	-171
1AB.	1822	1614	1408	1204	995	780	559	333	125	-67	-241	-398	-538	-440	-343	-171
B.C.	4207	3706	3209	2717	2230	1761	1324	918	543	199	-91	-329	-515	-440	-343	-171
D.E.	2600	2215	1834	1457	1084	714	348	16	-269	-506	-696	-840	-937	-693	-429	-213
2D.E.	1819	1442	1069	699	334	-28	-358	-639	-872	-1058	-1198	-1292	-1044	-777	-558	-341
AB.C.	4062	3562	3066	2576	2104	1656	1231	831	454	122	-163	-404	-391	-363	-266	-171
1AB.C.	3364	2870	2382	1911	1465	1043	644	269	-61	-345	-583	-568	-538	-440	-343	-171

Figure 11.9
Sequence Adjusted Net Present Values (SANPVs) at 1% per Period ($US in thousands)

- First, and unsurprisingly, the architectural elements have negative SANPVs because they have no independent returns.

- Second, the strands allow us to assess the combined NPV of a particular MMF with its architectural precursor(s). For example, although MMF A appears to be profitable if started anywhere up to and including period 13, it has an architectural precursor. Examining its profitability without taking this into account is futile. If instead we examine the **1A** strand we see the true profitability of MMF A: It only returns a positive NPV if the strand is started between periods 1 and 9.

- Third, the SANPV table allows us to see "through" individual MMFs to examine the financial attractiveness of a longer strand of development. For example, although the **1A** strand is profitable until period 9, the strand **1AB.C.** is only profitable until period 8.

Sequence Selection

In Chapter 5 we examined the issues surrounding sequence selection and discovered that selecting a sequence based on the maximization of immediate financial returns (the greedy approach) rarely optimizes the NPV. However, because the greedy approach has intuitive appeal we will reexamine it and compare the results to the more thorough IFM heuristic.

The greedy approach takes each MMF in turn, analyzes the NPV, and then implements the one that delivers the greatest return. In financial terms, it's a "short-termist" approach.

Initially we assume that development is constrained to a single MMF per quarter. Later in this chapter we demonstrate how the NPV could be improved and project-level objectives fulfilled through the concurrent development of MMFs.

The Greedy Heuristic

Because all of the MMFs in this example have at least one architectural precursor, comparing individual MMFs for immediate return would be misleading. So we'll start by examining strands of length two that consist of an AE followed by an MMF. This reflects the fact that the greedy approach has only a shortsighted perspective and ignores longer strands, such as **1AB.C.**. There are only three allowable strands to consider in period 1, and their NPVs can be found by examining the SANPV table in Figure 11.9. These period 1 strands are depicted in Figure 11.10a.

The strand **3F.** is the clear winner here. The greedy approach therefore starts with constructing AE 3, followed by MMF F. Development of this strand takes three periods (one for AE 3 and two for MMF F), meaning that the next sequencing decision should be made against period 4. The NPVs for strands in Figure 11.10b are therefore taken from column 4 of Figure 11.9 and represent all available selections for this period.

Strand **2D.** clearly has the most attractive SANPV in period 4, so AE 2 is scheduled for development in period 4, followed by MMF D in periods 5 and 6. The next available period is period 7, and the available options for this period are depicted in Figure 11.10 c.

These SANPVs indicate that the most attractive next step, in NPV terms, is to construct MMF E, which takes two periods and therefore consumes the two remaining periods of 7 and 8. The greedy approach then terminates because there are no further development periods available to us in this case study project.

The sequence recommended by the greedy heuristic is therefore **3F.2D.E.**

Rank	Strand	Period 1 NPV $K
1	3F.	1111
2	2D.	753
3	1A	155

a. SANPVs for elements available during period 1. **3F**. is selected and developed during periods 1, 2, and 3.

Rank	Strand	Period 4 NPV $K
1	2D.	279
2	1A	151

b. SANPVs for elements available during period 4. **2D.** is selected and developed during periods 4, 5, and 6.

Rank	Strand	Period 7 NPV $K
1	E.	420
2	1A	101

c. SANPVs for elements available during period 7. **E.** is selected and delivered during periods 7 and 8.

Figure 11.10
Sequencing Using the Greedy Approach

We'll evaluate this sequence later in the chapter to see just how effective it has been at optimizing NPV. But first we'll examine the sequence recommended by the IFM heuristic.

The IFM Heuristic

The SANPV table in Figure 11.9 conveys only part of the story. The longer strands consume more time and therefore prevent resources from being deployed on what may potentially be shorter and more profitable activities. We therefore weight our SANPV values according to their development duration as described in Chapter 5. In this example we've applied a weighting factor of 15%. The resulting time-weighted SANPVs (or WSANPVs) are illustrated in Figure 11.11.

The IFM heuristic uses this WSANPV table to select the most interesting strand. As described in Chapter 5, the objective of the heuristic is to optimize the NPV of the project *every period* by choosing the best possible strand with the highest NPV, provided it is valid against the precursors table. In this respect the IFM heuristic has the ability to look ahead, regardless of strand length.

Strand	Period															
	1	2	3	4	5	6	7	8	9	10	11	12	13	14	15	16
1	-198	-196	-194	-192	-190	-188	-187	-185	-183	-181	-179	-177	-176	-174	-172	-171
2	-396	-392	-388	-384	-381	-377	-373	-369	-366	-362	-359	-355	-351	-348	-345	-341
3	-198	-196	-194	-192	-190	-188	-187	-185	-183	-181	-179	-177	-176	-174	-172	-171
A	357	353	350	346	343	332	313	287	254	214	166	111	49	-20	-96	-171
1A	132	131	129	128	120	106	86	59	26	-13	-58	-109	-166	-229	-291	-145
B.	1773	1594	1417	1241	1068	896	725	557	390	224	80	-44	-147	-229	-291	-145
C.	2306	2053	1803	1556	1310	1068	828	601	400	224	72	-55	-158	-236	-291	-145
D.	1117	976	837	700	564	429	296	164	46	-58	-148	-224	-286	-335	-364	-181
E.	1472	1282	1093	906	722	539	357	178	0	-150	-274	-372	-444	-490	-510	-254
F.	1221	1112	1005	898	792	687	583	481	379	278	179	80	-17	-82	-146	-72
2D.	527	415	305	195	87	-20	-126	-221	-304	-375	-435	-484	-522	-544	-390	-239
3F.	777	690	603	518	433	349	265	183	101	21	-59	-139	-190	-242	-180	-119
AB.	1563	1414	1267	1122	977	829	678	522	363	215	80	-43	-154	-254	-186	-119
1AB.	1002	888	774	662	547	429	308	183	69	-37	-132	-219	-296	-242	-189	-94
B.C.	2314	2038	1765	1494	1226	969	728	505	299	110	-50	-181	-283	-242	-189	-94
D.E.	1430	1218	1009	801	596	393	192	9	-148	-278	-383	-462	-515	-381	-236	-117
2D.E.	728	577	428	280	133	-11	-143	-255	-349	-423	-479	-517	-418	-311	-223	-136
AB.C.	1625	1425	1227	1030	841	662	493	332	181	49	-65	-162	-156	-145	-106	-68
1AB.C.	841	718	595	478	366	261	161	67	-15	-86	-146	-142	-135	-110	-86	-43

Figure 11.11
15% Time-weighted SANPVs (WSANPVs) ($US in Thousands)

Let's examine the IFM heuristic in action.

We start by ranking the WSANPVs for each strand. Our table of ordered WSANPVs for each of the eight available development periods is depicted in Figure 11.12.

From the table we see that in period 1 the highest WSANPV comes from the strand **B.C.**. The second highest comes from **C.**. However, only strands that have no unfulfilled precursors are really available for development, which means that neither **B.C.** nor **C.** are available for selection. In fact, all strands with unfulfilled precursors must be filtered out, which significantly reduces the number of available strands in any individual period. In this example there are only nine strands that can be considered for development in period 1, and these are ranked in order of value in Figure 11.13a.

In this case, the period 1 strand with the best WSANPV returns is **1AB.**. This strand is therefore selected, and AE 1 is scheduled for development in period 1. Based on this selection, a slightly different set of strands is available for consideration in period 2. This set includes both the strands starting with AEs 2 and 3, and the strands starting with MMF A. From this set, **AB.C.** is selected, and MMF A is scheduled in period 2. The process continues as illustrated in Figure 11.13 until all delivery periods are filled. In the final scheduling tasks, depicted in Figure 11.13e, the only strand with positive WSANPV cannot be selected because it would take a total of three development periods and only two are actually available.

Rank / Period	1	2	3	4	5	6	7	8
1	B.C.	C.	C.	C.	C.	C.	C.	C.
2	C.	B.C.	B.C.	B.C.	B.C.	B.C.	B.C.	B.
3	B.	B.	B.	B.	B.	B.	B.	AB.
4	AB.C.	AB.C.	AB.	AB.	AB.	AB.	AB.	B.C.
5	AB.	AB.	AB.C.	AB.C.	AB.C.	F.	F.	F.
6	E.	E.	E.	E.	E.	AB.C.	AB.C.	AB.C.
7	D.E.	D.E.	D.E.	F.	F.	E.	E.	A
8	F.	F.	F.	D.E.	D.E.	D.	A	1AB.
9	D.	D.	D.	D.	D.	1AB.	1AB.	3F.
10	1AB.	1AB.	1AB.	1AB.	1AB.	D.E.	D.	E.
11	1AB.C.	1AB.C.	3F.	3F.	3F.	3F.	3F.	D.
12	3F.	3F.	1AB.C.	1AB.C.	1AB.C.	A	D.E.	1AB.C.
13	2D.E.	2D.E.	2D.E.	A	A	1AB.C.	1AB.C.	1A
14	2D.	2D.	A	2D.E.	2D.E.	1A	1A	D.E.
15	A	A	2D.	2D.	1A			
16	1A	1A	1A	1A	2D.			

Figure 11.12
Strands Ordered by Decreasing WSANPV for Each Period

Rank	Strand	Period 2 WSANPV
1	1AB	1002
2	1AB.C.	841
3	2D.E.	728
4	3F.	777
5	2D.	527
6	1A	132
7	3	-198
8	1	-198
9	2	-396

a. WSANPV for strands available during period 1. **1A** is selected and 1 is scheduled for period 1.

Rank	Strand	Period 2 WSANPV
1	AB.C.	1425
2	AB.	1414
3	3F.	690
4	2D.E.	577
5	2D.	415
6	A	353
7	3	-196
8	2	-392

b. WSANPV for strands available during period 2. **AB.C.** is selected and A is scheduled.

Rank	Strand	Period 3 WSANPV
1	B.C.	1765
2	B.	1417
3	3F.	603
4	2D.E.	428
5	2D.	305
6	3	-194
7	2	-388

c. SWANPV for strands available during period 3. **B.C.** is selected and B is scheduled for the two periods 3 and 4.

Rank	Strand	Period 3 WSANPV
1	C.	1310
2	3F.	433
3	2D.E.	133
4	2D.	87
5	3	-190
6	2	-381

d. WSANPV for strands available during the 5th period. **C.** is selected and scheduled for periods 5 and 6.

Rank	Strand	Period 3 WSANPV
1	3F.	265
2	2D.E.	-143
3	2D.	-126
4	3	-187
5	2	-373

e. WSANPV for strands available during the 7th period. No strands are selected because the only profitable strand will not "fit" into the remaining two development periods.

Figure 11.13
The Sequencing Process for the IFM Heuristic

The IFM heuristic therefore recommends the following sequence for optimizing the NPV of this case study project: **1AB.C.**

In summary, the IFM heuristic recommends implementing AE 1, followed by MMFs A, B, and C, and then stopping (a six-period sequence). We'll take the opportunity to examine how effective the heuristic has been in achieving optimized NPV shortly. Before doing this, we should consider a couple of interesting points.

- First, IFM has created a development sequence that does not construct all the AEs. It has in fact chosen to implement just one of them. In this respect IFM has adopted an agile approach, choosing only to create those AEs that are necessary and ignoring those that are not.

- Second, IFM has developed only a subset of the available MMFs. In the interests of optimizing NPV, MMFs D, E, and F have not been constructed. In a sense this is unsurprising, as there are only eight periods available for development in this particular study. However, IFM has applied financial rigor to the choice and ordering of those MMFs. We'll take the opportunity now to examine the effectiveness of that choice.

Following this discussion we reexamine the decision to develop only one MMF at a time, in order to determine how concurrent development might more effectively deliver the functionality requested by the bank within the available schedule.

Measuring the Effectiveness of the IFM Heuristic

The IFM heuristic is provided as an alternative to evaluating every possible sequence, the computational overhead of which is not feasible in complex projects. Fortunately, in this study the number of permissible sequences is only just over 400. This number is manageable enough to afford us the luxury of measuring the effectiveness of the heuristic against hard data. Figure 11.14 shows the highest-ranked sequences by NPV.

The sequence recommended by the IFM heuristic turns out to be the highest ranked of all sequences, indicating that the heuristic has been particularly effective in this case study.

While these results are certainly gratifying, it is important to recognize that the heuristic can only ever find an approximation of the optimal NPV. The reasons for this are discussed in Chapter 5.

As a point of comparison, the sequence recommended by the greedy heuristic, **3F.2D.E.** also appears in this table. It is suboptimal by $1,554 million and achieves only 54% of the maximum realizable NPV!

NPV Rank	Sequence	NPV $K	% Optimal	Suboptimal by $K
1	1AB.C.	3364	100%	0
2	1AB.C.3	3177	94%	187
3	1AB.C.2	2991	89%	373
4	1AB.C.32	2808	83%	556
5	1AB.C.23	2806	83%	558
6	1AB.2C.	2698	80%	666
7	13AB.C.	2672	79%	692
8	31AB.C.	2672	79%	692
9	1AB.2C.3	2513	75%	851
10	1A2B.C.	2484	74%	880
11	12AB.C.	2476	74%	888
12	21AB.C.	2474	74%	890
13	1AB.3F.	2440	73%	924
14	2D.E.3F.	2317	69%	1047
15	3F.1AB.	2315	69%	1049
16	13AB.C.2	2303	68%	1061
17	31AB.C.2	2303	68%	1061
18	1A2B.C.3	2299	68%	1065
19	12AB.C.3	2292	68%	1072
20	21AB.C.3	2290	68%	1074
21	1A3B.F.	2230	66%	1134
22	1A3B.32C.	2229	66%	1135
23	1AB.23C.	2227	66%	1137
24	13AB.F.	2224	66%	1139
25	31F.AB.	2184	65%	1180
26	13F.AB.	2184	65%	1180
27	2D.3E.F	2096	62%	1268
28	1AB.3F.2	2071	62%	1293
29	1A3F.B.	2071	62%	1293
30	13AF.B.	2065	61%	1299
31	31AB.2C.	2013	60%	1351
32	2D.1AB.	1957	58%	1407
33	3F.1AB.2	1945	58%	1418
34	2D.E.1A	1944	58%	1420
35	32D.E.F.	1930	57%	1433
36	23D.E.F.	1928	57%	1435
37	2D.3F.E.	1913	57%	1451
38	1A3B.F.2	1861	55%	1503
39	13AB.F.2	1855	55%	1509
40	1AB.	1822	54%	1542

Figure 11.14
Sequences with the Highest NPV

It's also interesting to examine the sequences for which all the architectural elements are constructed first. The highest-ranking such sequence in the table is **321AB.C.** It has an NPV of only $1,792 million, which is just 53%

NPV Rank	Sequence	NPV $K	% Optimal	Suboptimal by $K
41	2D.E.	1819	54%	1545
42	31F.AB.2	1815	54%	1549
43	12F.AB.2	1815	54%	1549
44	3F.2D.E.	1810	54%	1554
45	31A2B.C.	1801	54%	1563
46	13A2B.C.	1801	54%	1563
47	312AB.C.	1794	53%	1570
48	321AB.C.	1792	53%	1572
49	12D.AB.	1791	53%	1572
50	2D.1AB.3	1772	53%	1592

Figure 11.14, continued
Sequences with the Highest NPV

of optimal. The IFM analysis has therefore brought some clarity and rigor to the debate between traditional and agile methodologies. In this particular case, the financial impact of instantiating all AEs up front as opposed to adopting a more agile approach, is severe. It has also distracted from valuable development time, in that AEs were constructed for which the corresponding MMFs were not developed, due to lack of time.

ROI Analysis

We can also perform an ROI analysis for our selected sequence using the techniques identified in Chapter 2. The IFM elements table in Figure 11.8 give us the information to allow an ROI over the 16 periods to be calculated, as demonstrated in Figure 11.15.

Sequence	Element	1	2	3	4	5	6	7	8	9	10	11	12	13	14	15	16	Net
1AB.C.	1	-200	0	0	0	0	0	0	0	0	0	0	0	0	0	0	0	-200
	A		-200	90	90	81	72	63	54	45	36	27	18	9	0	0	0	385
	B			-200	-200	90	117	144	171	198	225	225	225	225	225	225	225	1,895
	.																	
	C					-200	-200	80	112	144	176	208	240	272	304	320	320	1,776
Cash		-200	-200	-110	-110	-29	-11	287	337	387	437	460	483	506	529	545	545	3,856
Investment		-200	-200	-110	-110	-29	-11											-660
ROI																		584%

Figure 11.15
ROI analysis for IFM Heuristic Sequence ($US in Thousands)

If the project is developed using this sequence recommended by the IFM heuristic, the business must provide $660,000 to fund the project over six periods. Thereafter the project is self-funding and returns $3,364 million over the analysis period, yielding a very healthy ROI of 584%.

Cash Flow and Breakeven Time

Although NPV comparisons measure the attractiveness of the financial return of a development sequence, cash-flow considerations are likely to dictate whether a particular sequence is financially feasible. For example, if the sequence with the optimal NPV results in a cash-flow position that is unsustainable in mid-sequence, it may be necessary to revert to a sequence with a lower NPV in order to ensure a more fundable cash flow.

From an investment perspective we want to break even as early as possible. Once the breakeven point is reached, the project is returning real value.

We can calculate the discounted cash flow as shown in Figure 11.16.

Figure 11.17 shows the top sequences ranked by breakeven time. It reveals that the development sequence has an NPV of $3,364 million and breaks even in just over nine periods.

As an aside, this kind of analysis can be applied to a number of potentially interesting sequences in order to obtain a ranking by breakeven time. We've also included the lowest value of the rolling NPV in the table (designated "MaxDebt") to provide an indication of the discounted cost of funding the sequence.

If we take a look at the sequence recommended by the IFM heuristic, **1AB.C.**, we see that although it has the highest NPV it is not the sequence

Sequence	Element	1	2	3	4	5	6	7	8	9	10	11	12	13	14	15	16	Net
1AB.C.	1	-200	0	0	0	0	0	0	0	0	0	0	0	0	0	0	0	-200
	A		-200	90	90	81	72	63	54	45	36	27	18	9	0	0	0	385
	B			-200	-200	90	117	144	171	198	225	225	225	225	225	225	225	1,895
	.																	
	C					-200	-200	80	112	144	176	208	240	272	304	320	320	1,776
Cash		-200	-200	-110	-110	-29	-11	287	337	387	437	460	483	506	529	545	545	3,856
PV @ 1%		-198	-196	-107	-106	-28	-10	268	311	354	396	412	429	445	460	469	465	3,364
Rolling NPV		-198	-394	-501	-607	-634	-645	-377	-66	288	684	1,096	1,525	1,969	2,430	2,899	3,364	
Breakeven									X									9.19

Figure 11.16
Discounted Cash Flow for IFM Heuristic Sequence ($US in Thousands)

Rank	Sequence	Breakeven Time (Periods)	Max Debt ($K)	NPV ($K)
1	3F.	7.75	-393	1111
2	1A	8.33	-394	155
3	1AB.	8.35	-607	1822
4	3F.1A	8.91	-603	1261
5	1AB.C.	9.19	-645	3364
6	1AB.3	9.25	-634	1632
7	3F.1	9.29	-499	919
8	1A3F.	9.36	-529	1017
9	1AB.3F.	9.52	-634	2440
10	13F.A	9.60	-692	1130

Figure 11.17
Sequences Ranked by Breakeven Time

with the best breakeven time. In fact, it ranks only fifth in breakeven terms. On the other hand, the sequence **3F.** breaks even in only 7.75 periods and it is exceedingly cheap to fund (about half the cost of the sequence recommended by the IFM heuristic). However, its NPV is dismal, at only just over $1 million.

Concurrent Development

As it stands, the identified schedule delivers about half of the requested functionality within the eight-period development window. This situation could, however, be remedied by concurrent development.

To identify a parallel delivery sequence, the IFM look-ahead algorithm is applied in the same way as the previous example, except that multiple elements (MMFs and AEs) may be selected for a single period. In reality, the problem of selecting MMFs and AEs for development is constrained by the availability of specific resources, such as skilled personnel. It is as much a project-management issue as a funding issue. IFM simply identifies the most financially lucrative MMFs to develop; it does not provide resource management for determining whether specific resources will be available.

For example, if IFM suggested that a certain MMF would be the best option for the next period, the project manager could either accept or reject these suggestions based on availability of development resources. If, for example, the MMF required very specific skills unavailable in the current period, it could be delayed and the next-best one selected from the WSAN-PV table.

As discussed at the end of Chapter 5, there are two types of relationships in the precursor table. The first requires strict sequential development of MMFs within a strand, while the second allows parallel development. In other words, given a strand **AB**, the former situation would require MMF A to be developed in one period and MMF B in a later period, while the latter situation would allow both MMFs A and B to be developed during the same period, with the understanding that MMF B would not be able to be deployed until MMF A was completed.

In our case study, if we assume the need for strict sequential development, the selection process depicted in Figure 11.18 will occur.

The identified parallel delivery sequence is summarized in Figure 11.19.

Rank	Strand	Period 1 WSANPV
1	1AB	1002
2	1AB.C.	841
3	2D.E.	728
4	3F.	777
5	2D.	527
6	1A	132
7	3	-198
8	1	-198
9	2	-396

a. WSANPV for strands available during period 1. **1A** is selected and AE-1 is scheduled for period 1. **2D.E.** is also selected, and AE-2 is scheduled.

Rank	Strand	Period 2 WSANPV
1	AB.C.	1625
2	AB.	1563
3	D.E.	1430
4	D.	1117
5	3F.	777
6	A	357
7	3	-198

b. WSANPV for strands available during period 2. **AB.C.** is selected and A is scheduled for period 2. Also D is selected and scheduled for periods 2 and 3.

Rank	Strand	Period 3 WSANPV
1	B.C.	1765
2	B.	1417
3	3F.	603
4	3	-194

c. SANPV for strands available during period 3. D is still under development so only one additional element can be selected. **B.C.** is selected and B is scheduled for the two periods 3 and 4.

Rank	Strand	Period 4 WSANPV
1	E.	1093
2	3F.	518
3	3	-192

d. WSANPV for strands available during the 4th period. B is still under development so only one additional element can be selected. **E.** is selected and scheduled for periods 4 and 5.

Figure 11.18
Concurrent Sequencing with the IFM Heuristic

Rank	Strand	Period 5 WSANPV
1	C.	1310
2	3F.	433
3	3	-190

Rank	Strand	Period 6 WSANPV
1	3F.	349
2	3	-188

f. Strand **3F.** is selected and AE-3 is scheduled for period 6.

e. WSANPV for strands available during the 5th period. E is still under development so only one additional element can be selected. **C.** is selected and scheduled for periods 5 and 6.

Rank	Strand	Period 7 WSANPV
1	F.	583

g. The remaining strand **F.** is selected and scheduled for development in periods 7 and 8.

Figure 11.18, continued
Concurrent Sequencing with the IFM Heuristic

The IFM financial analysis of this parallel delivery sequence appears in Figure 11.20.

We now have a parallel sequence that has an impressive NPV of $5.797 million, and the entire functionality is developed within the two-year development window. This benefit comes at a price however—the sequence costs $2.205 million to fund (in sharp contrast to the figure of only $660,000 to fund the serial sequence). In addition, the ROI is reduced to 307% and the breakeven point is delayed, to 10.72 periods. The business may or may not decide to implement parallelization in the light of these figures. Nonetheless, IFM has provided the information needed to ensure than an informed decision can be made.

Development Thread	Period							
	1	2	3	4	5	6	7	8
(i)	1	A	B	•	C	•	F	•
(ii)	2	D	•	E	•	3		

Figure 11.19
Two-thread Parallel Delivery Sequence

Sequence	Element	1	2	3	4	5	6	7	8	9	10	11	12	13	14	15	16	Net
1AB.C.F.	1	-200	0	0	0	0	0	0	0	0	0	0	0	0	0	0	0	-200
	A		-200	90	90	81	72	63	54	45	36	27	18	9	0	0	0	385
	B			-200	-200	90	117	144	171	198	225	225	225	225	225	225	225	1,895
	.																	
	C					-200	-200	80	112	144	176	208	240	272	304	320	320	1,776
	.																	
	F							-100	-100	90	90	135	135	135	135	135	135	790
	.																	
2E.D.3	2	-400	0	0	0	0	0	0	0	0	0	0	0	0	0	0	0	-400
	E		-350	-350	35	70	105	140	175	210	245	245	245	245	245	245	245	1,750
	.																	
	D				-250	-250	-45	72	90	108	126	144	162	180	180	180	180	967
	.																	
	3						-200	0	0	0	0	0	0	0	0	0	0	-200
Cash		-600	-550	-460	-325	-209	-61	399	502	795	898	984	1,025	1,066	1,089	1,105	1,105	6,763
Investment		-600	-550	-460	-325	-209	-61											-2,205
ROI																		307%
PV @ 1%		-594	-539	-446	-312	-199	-57	372	464	727	813	882	910	937	947	952	942	5,797
Rolling NVP		-594	-1,133	-1,580	-1,892	-2,091	-2,148	-1,776	-1,313	-586	227	1,109	2,019	2,956	3,903	4,855	5,797	
Breakeven										X								10.72

Figure 11.20
Financial Analysis of Parallel Sequence

Summary

This chapter provided a more complete example of IFM in action. The example of the Web-facing banking portal illustrated the benefits of applying a more rigorous financial analysis to the sequencing of a software application project. The following points were discussed:

- Although self-funding is desirable, optimizing for breakeven time is unwise because it can result in suboptimal NPV. The approach taken by IFM is to optimize for NPV instead. The IFM heuristic provides a way to approximate optimal NPV without having to compute and calculate all available sequences.

- Once the optimal sequence has been defined, its cash flow should be analyzed to check that the business is able to fund it. If the sequence is nonfundable, a sequence with suboptimal NPV but more favorable funding requirements may be selected instead.

- Extrapolating against the discounted cash flow (typically through linear regression) yields an accurate breakeven time. IFM allows the business to predict when the project will reach this point.

- IFM enables project stakeholders to identify financially viable parts of the system. This provides a clear business objective for the development of the selected MMFs, and enables stakeholders to reject MMFs that will not return significant returns.

- Parallel development sequences can also be elicited through use of the IFM heuristic. In some cases parallel development will be desirable, but budget and resource constraints are likely to determine the extent to which parallelization is possible. Nevertheless, IFM provides visibility into the financial impact of parallel development options and thus continues to deliver an ROI-informed approach.

Appendix A
Summary of IFM Terminology

Architectural Element (AE): The architecture of a software system is decomposed into an assembly of smaller pieces known as architectural elements. Unlike a minimum marketable feature (MMF), which returns revenue, an AE is treated purely as a cost element. By factoring architectural costs into the sequencing cost base, the incremental funding methodology (IFM) ensures that architecture is subject to the same cost-benefit analysis as all other aspects of software development. IFM uses sequencing strategies to identify the optimal time for instantiating each piece of the architecture. The objective is to develop architectural components as they are needed to support the functionality of each MMF, while optimizing the financial returns of the project.

Breakeven Time: The breakeven time is the point in a project's timeline at which the accumulated investment has been paid back by project-generated revenues.

Discounted Cash Flow (DCF): The discounted cash flow is the set of present-value corrected cash positions (see NPV).

Incremental Funding Methodology (IFM): The incremental funding methodology is an ROI-informed approach in which software is developed and delivered in carefully prioritized chunks of customer-valued functionality, called *minimum marketable features* (MMFs). IFM integrates traditional software engineering activities with financially informed project management strategies. IFM heuristics provide clarity into important metrics such as project-level NPV, ROI, initial start-up investment costs, and time needed for a project to reach self-funding status. It enables developers, customers, and business stakeholders to answer critical questions related to the development and delivery of a product and to optimize strategies accordingly. In short, IFM equips developers and project managers with techniques and principles for increasing the financial returns of a software project and for identifying development schedules that make a project financially feasible.

IFM Heuristic (Weighted Look-Ahead Algorithm): The IFM heuristic is a set of rules that guide the developer in selecting an optimal sequencing strategy for the MMFs and AEs of a project. The IFM heuristic identifies MMFs for development by comparing the net present value (NPV) of available substrands. A weighting factor is applied to substrands that take longer to develop. The IFM heuristic identifies the delivery sequence that returns near-optimal project-level NPV without the overhead of calculating the NPV of all possible sequences. Sequencing decisions are revisited prior to each MMF iteration.

Minimum Marketable Feature (MMF): A minimum marketable feature is a chunk of functionality that delivers a subset of the customer's requirements, and that is capable of returning value to the customer when released as an independent entity. The value of an MMF can be defined in a number of ways, including tangible factors such as revenue generation and cost savings, and less tangible factors such as competitive differentiation, brand-name projection, and enhanced customer loyalty.

MMF Precedence Graph: The development and delivery of MMFs and AEs can be constrained by many factors related to the business needs of the customer and developmental dependencies of the software itself. These constraints are captured as precursor dependencies in an MMF precedence graph. A series of dependent MMFs and AEs in the precedent graph is known as a *strand*, and a section of a strand is known as a *substrand*.

Net Present Value (NPV): The current value of future cash can be estimated by discounting it against an assumed interest rate. This calculates the present value (PV) of the future cash. At an interest rate of i% the present value of \$x in n years' time is defined as follows: $PV = x / (1 + i/100)^n$.

The discounted cash flow of the project can then be calculated by taking the cash position for each time period and applying PV corrections. The sum of these positions is known as the *net present value* (NPV). Given an annual discount rate of i and n periods per year, then the discount rate per period is calculated as: $n\sqrt{(1 + i/100)}$.

Self-Funding Status: A project reaches self-funding status when it no longer needs cash injections from the business to sustain it.

Sequence: The IFM heuristic identifies a delivery sequence that optimizes project-level characteristics such as ROI and NPV. The sequence represents the ordering in which MMFs and AEs will be developed and delivered to the customer. The same notation used to represent a strand is adopted to represent a sequence in which a period is used to depict an additional development period (see Strand). Concurrent development projects are represented as multiple sequences.

Sequence-Adjusted Net Present Values (SANPVs): Each MMF and AE is represented as a table of costs and revenues over the project's analysis period. IFM calculates the NPV of each MMF for each possible starting period in the project lifecycle. In IFM these position-dependent NPVs are called *sequence-adjusted net present values* (SANPVs). An SANPV for an MMF in period P therefore defines the NPV of that MMF if its development were to start in period P.

Strand: A strand is a series of dependent MMFs and AEs that form a path within the precedence graph. For example, if MMF C is dependent on MMF B, MMF B is dependent on MMF A, and MMF A is dependent on AE 1, these MMFs and AE form a strand, depicted as **1ABC**. A period is used after the MMF or AE name to depict an additional development period. **1A.BC** therefore represents this same strand but specifies that MMF A takes two periods to develop. Similarly, the strand **1A..BC** would specify that MMF A takes three periods to develop.

Substrand: A strand can be divided into smaller sections such as **A**, **AB**, or **BCD**. These sections of the strand are called *substrands*.

Appendix B

Quick Guide to the Incremental Funding Method

1. Define project-level strategies, such as length of the development and analysis phases, duration of each development and analysis period, and applicable discount rate.

2. Identify candidate MMFs and evaluate them according to their ability to return value in terms of revenue generation, cost savings, competitive differentiation, brand-name projection, enhanced customer loyalty, and other identified criterion. (See Chapter 3.)

3. Define cost and revenue figures for all tangible MMFs. (See Chapter 3.)

4. Evaluate equivalency values for intangible MMFs. (See Chapter 7.)

5. If a traditional software development process such as RUP is being used, evaluate and select an architecture and decompose it into AEs. Construct cost figures for each AE. (See Chapter 4.)

6. Consider business and developmental dependencies between MMFs and AEs, and construct an MMF precedence graph for them. (See Chapter 4.)

7. Construct an SANPV table for each MMF and AE. (See Chapter 3.)

8. Select an appropriate weighting factor according to specific project characteristics. A table of weighting factors is available online at http://softwarebynumbers.org. Weight the values in the SANPV table according to the appropriate weighting factors. (See Chapter 5.)

9. Apply the IFM heuristics to identify the optimal delivery sequence(s). (See Chapter 5 and/or download the IFM tool from http://softwarebynumbers.org.)

10. Examine critical project metrics, such as maximum cash injection needed, time to self-funding, time to break-even, and project-level ROI. If necessary, apply the techniques described in Chapter 10 to manipulate these project level characteristics in order to create a fundable project.

Index

A

Agile development, 28
  architecture defined, 44
  incremental funding methodology and
    benefits to, 122–123
  misconceptions of, 122
  simple versus look-ahead solution, 134–139
*Agile Software Development: Principles, Patterns,
  and Practices* (Martin), 132
Alexander, Christopher, 45, 46
Application service providers (ASPs), 154–155
Architectural elements (AEs), 50
  case example, 161–163
  constructing, 116–118
  sequencing, 74–75, 113–114
Architecture
  codependency, 48–49
  coherency, 54–55
  decomposition, 50–52
  defined, 43–44
  dependency sequencing, 53–54, 163
  eXtreme programming, 44, 132–133
  lifecycle, 112–113
  multiple inheritance, 55–57
  problem with, 45–46
  selecting, 110–111
  spiral, 57, 104
  tradeoff analysis method (ATAM), 111
  usefulness, 46–47
  value-driven approach, 47
  versus rules, 44–45

B

Bass, L., 43, 45
Beck, Kent, 122
Behavior, categories of, 79–81
Boehm, Barry, 3, 36, 47, 57, 115
Booch, G., 45
Bottom-up approach, 31, 36

Breakeven time, 16, 18, 19, 147–148, 176–180
Business case, 15, 106
Busse, K., 46

C

Capablanca Y Granperra, J. R., 56
Cash flow projections, 15–16, 176–180
Chaos Report, 106, 112
Clements, P., 43, 45
Coad, Peter, 3
Codependency, architecture, 48–49
Coherency, architecture, 54–55
Construction, 116–118
Constructive cost model (COCOMO), 36, 37, 57
Cost-benefit analysis
  case example, 164–166
  of delivery sequence, 63–66
  of intangibles, 97–99
Costs
  of developing minimum marketable features,
    36–37
  estimating, 111–112
  lost opportunity, 100–101
  versus value analysis, 62–63
Customer
  requirements, 10
  voice of, 10

D

Dataquest CIO, 14
Decision making, 10
  collaboration, need for, 145–146
  getting a project funded, 146–148
  project characteristics, manipulating, 149–150
Decomposition
  See also Function-class decomposition
  architecture, 50–52
  of minimum marketable features into use
    cases, 107–108

Delivery
  cost-benefit analysis of, 63–66
  parallel development, 83–87
  time-sensitive, 81–82
Dependency sequencing, architecture, 53–54
Design, 114–116
Development time, 37
Discounted cash flow (DCF), 17–18, 19
Dollar amounts, translating value to, 32–34

E

Elaboration, 110–113
eXtreme programming (XP), 3, 122
  architecture defined, 44, 132–133
  release, 123–124, 127–129
  user stories, 124–129
Extreme Programming Explained: Embrace Change (Beck), 122
Extreme Programming Explored (Wake), 127

F

Feature
  design, 116
  operational capability, 117
  release, 118
  use of term, 29
Feature-driven development (FDD), 3, 29, 122, 140–142
Function-class decomposition, 30–31
Funding of a project, getting, 146–148

G

General Electric (GE), 9
Gilb, Tom, 57, 151
Glossary, developing a project, 109
Green Door Services, 3
Growth patterns, 82–83
Guadagno, L., 143

H

Hecksel, D., 46

I

IBM, 151
Inception, 105–110
Incremental funding methodology (IFM), 8, 27–28
  See also Agile development; Rational unified process; Sequencing strategies
  architectural elements, 50
  benefits to management, 155
  coherency, 54–55

decomposition, 50–52
heuristic, 170–175
impact of, 153–155
implementing, 152
multiple inheritance, 55–57
unexpected, dealing with the, 155–157
window, 151–152
Incremental funding methodology (IFM), case example
  architectural elements, eliciting, 161–163
  case flow and breakeven time, 176–180
  computation phase, 166–173
  dependencies, defining, 163
  financial phase, 164–166
  heuristic, 170–175
  minimum marketable features, selecting, 160–161
  minimum marketable feature strands, defining, 161
  precedence graph, construction of, 163–164
  return on investment analysis, 175–176
Information Week, 34
Initial operational capability (ICO), 117
Intangible(s)
  benefits, 34–35, 90
  cost-benefit analysis and, 97–99
  defined, 89
  hybrid, 97
  lost opportunity costs, 100–101
  managing, 90–91
  net present value, 99
  pairwise comparisons, 91, 92–97
Internal rate of return (IRR), 18–19

J

Jackson, I., 45
Java 2 Enterprise Edition (J2EE), 44

K

Kazman, R., 43, 45

L

Lee, C., 129
Lifecycle architecture (LCA), 112–113
Lifecycle objective (LCO), 109–110
Lost opportunity costs, 100–101

M

Marketable, use of term, 29
Martin, Robert, 132
Microsoft .Net, 44

Minimum marketable features (MMFs), 5
    behavior, categories of, 79–81
    candidate, 30–31
    construction, 116–118
    cost-benefit analysis of delivery sequence, 63–66
    costs of developing, 36–37
    decompose, into use cases, 107–108
    defined, 28–30
    design, 114–116
    development and delivery, 113–114
    elicit, 106–107
    graph, constructing, 108
    how value is created, 6
    hybrid, 97
    precedence graph, 38–39
    precursors, 37–38, 40
    return on investment, 22–24
    risk control and, 9
    risk factors and, 35–36, 108–109
    selecting, 6–7, 119, 160–161
    sequencing architectural elements and, 74–75,
        113–114
    time needed to develop, 37
    transition, 118
    user stories, 124–127
    value, determining, 31–37
Minimum marketable feature sequencing
        strategies
    greedy approach, 67–69, 168–170
    simple look-ahead approach, 69–72
    weighted look-ahead approach, 73–74, 170–173
Motorola, 9
Multiple inheritance, 55–57

N

Net present value (NPV), 17–18, 19, 114
    baseline, 99
    lost opportunity costs, 100–101
    potential, 99
    release plan and assessment of, 129–131
    sequence-adjusted (SANPVs), 33–34, 37,
        95–97, 129–131, 166–168
Next move principle, 56–57
Nonfunctional requirements (NFRs), 115

O

Object Management Group, 44

P

Pairwise comparisons, 91, 92–97
Parallel development, 83–87

Payback time, 16
Perry, D. E., 45
Plans, mini, 115–116
Precedence graph, 38–39, 163–164
Precursors, 37–38, 40
Prepayment period, 147
Present value (PV), 17, 19
Principles of Software Engineering Management
        (Gilb), 57, 151
Project characteristics, manipulating, 149–150
Project funding, getting, 146–148

R

Rational unified process (RUP), 3
    architecture defined, 44
    elaboration, 110–113
    inception, 105–110
    minimum marketable feature construction,
        116–118
    minimum marketable feature design, 114–116
    minimum marketable feature development
        and delivery, 113–114
    phases of incremental funding methodology
        compared to, 103–105
Release, 118
    assessment of net present value, 129–131
    eXtreme programming and, 123–124
    planning meetings, 131–132
    user stories and, 127–129
Return on investment (ROI)
    applications, 13–14
    breakeven time, 16, 18, 19
    business case, 15, 106
    case example, 175–176
    cash flow projections, 15–16
    defined, 19
    example, 19–21
    importance of, 14
    internal rate of return, 18–19
    minimum marketable feature, 22–24
    net present value, 17–18, 19
    payback time, 16
    present value, 17, 19
    traditional, 4
Risk
    control, 8–9, 24–25
    factors with minimum marketable features,
        35–36, 108–109
    sequencing and mitigation of, 76
Rules/standards, 44–45
Rumbaugh, J., 45

S

SCRUM, 122, 142
Self-funding status, 16, 19
Sequence-adjusted net present values (SANPVs), 33–34, 37, 95–97, 129–131, 166–168
Sequencing strategies
    See also Minimum marketable feature sequencing strategies
    architectural elements and, 74–75, 113–114
    cost-benefit analysis of delivery, 63–66
    cost versus value analysis, 62–63
    reevaluation of, 76
    risk mitigation, 76
Six Sigma approach, 9–11
Software Architecture in Practice (Bass, Clements, and Kazman), 43
Software development
    failure of, 1–3
    lack of customer involvement and failure of, 7–8
Spiral architecture, 57, 104
Story coupling, 129
Sun Microsystems, 9
    SunTone Architecture Methodology, 3, 46–47

T

Theory-W, 115
Time, development, 37
Timeless Way of Building, The (Alexander), 45

Top-down approach, 30–31
Transition, 118

U

Unified Modelling Language (UML), 45
Use cases, 107–108
User stories
    clustering, 124–127
    releases and, 127–129

V

Value
    cost versus analysis of, 62–63
    determining, 31–37
Vision statement, 106

W

Wake, Bill, 127
Waterfall approach, 4
Wolf, A. L., 45
Work-breakdown structure (WBS), 36, 37, 129

X

Xiaoping, J., 129
XP. *See* eXtreme programming

Z

Zierden, Troy, 13